Walk!

Mallorca

(North & Mountains)

with

Charles Davis

DISCOVERY WALKING GUIDES LTD

Walk! Mallorca (North & Mountains)
First published June 2004
Second Edition published January 2006
Reprinted March 2007
Third Edition published March 2009
Reprinted November 2010

Copyright © 2004, 2006, 2009, 2010

Published by
Discovery Walking Guides Ltd
10 Tennyson Close, Northampton NN5 7HJ,
England

Maps
Maps sections are taken from **Mallorca (North &
Mountains) Tour & Trail Map** 5th Edition,
ISBN 9781904946502 by **David Brawn** for
Discovery Walking Guides Ltd

Photographs
Photographs in this book were taken by the author,
Charles Davis, and Jeanette Tallegas.

Front Cover Photographs
Es Horts (Walk 46)   Coll de l'Ofre (Walk 14)

Views over Port de   **La Mola (Walk 45)**
    Sóller (Walk 1)

ISBN 9781904946496

All rights reserved. No part of this publication may
be reproduced, stored in a retrieval system or
transmitted in any form or by any means,
electronic, mechanical, photocopying, recording
or otherwise, without the prior written permission
of the publishers.

The author and
publishers have tried to
ensure that the
information and maps
in this publication are
as accurate as possible.
However, we accept no
responsibility for any
loss, injury or
inconvenience
sustained by anyone
using this book.

Walk! Mallorca
(North & Mountains)
CONTENTS

Charles Davis was born in London, and has lived and worked in the United States, Sudan, Turkey, Ivory Coast, Spain and France. With the onset of middle age, he realised that the urge to roam was better satisfied by walking than bouncing about on the back of a lorry in the middle of the desert, and now divides his time between mountain tops, desk-tops and laptops.

Jeanette Tallegas has spent thirty odd years labouring for the French education system, from which she has finally, gleefully, taken early retirement. Asked what she intends doing now, she resolutely replies, "Nothing". Nonetheless, she does follow the author up various gruelling mountains, frequently alarming younger walkers who seem to assume that remote and inaccessible places are the preserve of youth.

Charles Davis is also author of:-

GR221 Mallorca's Long Distance Walking Route
    ISBN 9781904946489
Walk! the Alpujarras
    ISBN 9781904946236
Walk! Mallorca West
    ISBN 9781899554980
Walk! La Gomera
    ISBN 9781899554904
Walk! La Palma
    ISBN 9781904946687
Walk! Andorraa
    ISBN 9781904946045
Walk! the Axarquía
    ISBN 9781904946656
Walk! the Lake District South
    ISBN 9781904946168

Walk! Dorset
    ISBN 9781904946205
Walk! Brittany (North)
    ISBN 9781904946359
Bumping About Brittany
    ISBN 9781904946441

- all published by
Discovery Walking Guides Ltd

- and by other publishers:-
Walk On, Bright Boy
ISBN 9781579621537 Permanent Press
Walking The Dog
ISBN 9781579621674 Permanent Press
Costa del Sol Walks
ISBN 8489954399 Santana
Costa Blanca Walks
ISBN 9788489954571 Santana

Preface to the 3rd Edition

It's always risky returning to places you've loved in the past, never more so than when the place in question is a walking destination with a history of disputes between landowners and hikers, so it was with some trepidation that we went back to Mallorca to update the present publication and research a new guide to the GR221.

We needn't have worried. Indeed, readers' letters over the years had suggested our itineraries were proving remarkably resilient. There have, of course, been negative changes, including the closure of longstanding permissive paths and the posting of Prohibido el Paso signs or the locking of gates on public paths and rightsofway. On the whole, though, the news from Mallorca for walkers is good, some of it very good.

The majority of landowners are still publicspirited enough to let people traipse across their land (one might even say forbearing enough given the numbers on some routes), Mallorcan ramblers continue to do great things (clearing paths, protesting against closures, and participating in mass 'trespasses' when required), the government has purchased several new estates to guarantee public access, some routes on which access had been restricted in recent years have reopened, and above all, new paths are being made staying in Sóller while writing up the results of our researches, I had the impression that everytime I took the dogs out for a walk, I discovered a new path! The chances are that if you like walking in Mallorca, you'll love what's happened recently. For so long, it seemed the story was going to be one of increasing restriction, but from some perspectives one can now assert the opposite.

The intention throughout this revision has been to produce enough new or substantially altered walks to make the 3rd edition a worthwhile purchase for people who have already visited the island several times, but would like to return for another dedicated walking holiday. Apart from checking access to extant itineraries and revising certain routes and descriptions according to the suggestions of readers, eleven itineraries have been rewalked in order to incorporate new paths, variants proposed by readers, or to check that tricky trails had not been completely overgrown, and eight new walks have been incorporated. I have not rewalked itineraries I knew were still valid just to take note of the new signposts the authorities have installed.

To minimize the risk of confusion and help purchasers of previous editions with cross referencing, new walks appear under the number of the itineraries they replace, even when this might suggest a slight geographical inconsistency. To see what's new, check out the contents list. NEW WALKS are obviously new walks! REVISED walks have been rewalked in part or whole, but have not substantially changed. NEW VERSIONS are variants on old walks that are sufficiently different to be worth doing again.

Acknowledgements

Previous acknowledgements remain valid, in many instances more than ever, but on the occasion of this, the 3rd edition of Walk! Mallorca North & Mountains, I would like to thank above all the readers whose feedback and comments have been so helpful. In particular, John Roper, Peter & Alysoun Dungworth, Des Sharratt, Clive Allen, Simon Barber, Richard Smithson, Carl Maxon, Ian & Elly Andison, David Gibbons, Anne Evans, Eva Smith, C.J.H. Low, Mike and Wendy Roach, and the technofile (name sadly lost) who sent us all those map coordinates for the Muleta plateau thank you, one and all. Please, don't feel slighted if you wrote in and your name doesn't feature here; the oversight is a consequence of rubbish file keeping on my part, not a conscious snub.

If you're at your wits end, or think you are, which amounts to the same thing, if you're dazed and confused by the noise of civilisation and the haste to get someplace where you find you have nothing to do, if busyness has swamped your brain with facts and science blinded you with gimmickry, then follow me to an island where calm reigns, where the men never hurry and the women never age, and even the sun and the moon move at a more leisurely pace: thus, paraphrased for the new millennium, begins 'La Illa de la Calma', the famous celebration of Mallorca by the modernist painter and writer Santiago Rusiñol. Perhaps the men move a little faster nowadays and doubtless the women age like everyone else, but the need for respite is more acute than ever and Rusiñol's evocation of tranquillity is as true today as it was eighty years ago. Forget the clichés about cluttered resorts catering to mass tourism; forget package holidays where it's the client rather than the services that are packaged; forget the crowded concrete tower blocks and beaches crammed with baking bodies; Mallorca has reinvented itself and, in so doing, has recovered its original face, the stillness and beauty of which have enchanted generations of artists and writers, and have now turned the island into Europe's most popular warm island walking destination.

THE ISLAND

As with so much that is praiseworthy in Spain, we have Africa to thank for the Balearics, which are in effect the exposed tip of the Baetic Cordillera, squeezed out of the earth's crust during the middle Tertiary period when pressure from the African plate occasioned all manner of happy havoc along southern Europe's tectonic frontiers. Subsequent folding, faulting, and karstic erosion have moulded this raw material into a tormented landscape of sheer cliffs and deep holes, weirdly fluted rocks, razor sharp ridges and fissured limestone pavement. What nature provided man has perfected, dappling the austere rockscape with groves of olive, almond and orange trees, taming precipitous slopes with neat terracing, canalising springs and streams, building remote mountain farms and beguiling sanctuaries, and gathering in picturesque fishing hamlets and atmospheric villages, all of which are linked by a complex network of paths pioneered by farm-labourers, muleteers, pilgrims, charcoal-burners, lime-firers, and snow-gatherers. The last three are particularly important for us, as these were the rural industries that penetrated the more inaccessible corners of the island, leaving their brand not only in paths but in the form of *sitjes*, circular moss-covered charcoal hearths, partially interred *hornos de calç* or lime kilns, and *casas de nieve* (*casa neu* in Catalan) or snow-pits. A less constructive but more lucrative business that also left its mark was piracy, which lead to the construction of the coastal watchtowers that provide a focal point for several classic Mallorcan walks.

The variety of walks that has resulted from all this fervid historical activity is remarkable, ranging from gentle strolls down peaceful country lanes, through bucolic rambles on cobbled donkey trails and pretty canal paths, to pathless scrambles traversing dense woods, rough scree, deep gullies, and remote windswept plateaux. Walking in Mallorca, we wind through pine forested slopes above azure blue waters, enter narrow gorges with towering walls that nearly touch high above our heads, peer over gratifyingly frightful precipices, marvel at dizzying sea views, discover idyllic creeks where swimming seems not so much desirable as compulsory, encounter rock formations so artfully sculpted you'd swear they were carved by hand, and admire olive trees so old and gnarled they look like stage-props from a computer-generated fantasy film… In short, if you can't find a walk to suit your tastes in Mallorca, you may as well hang up your boots and take to gardening!

The best known walking area is the **Serra Tramuntana** stretching from **Valldemossa** to **Pollença**, and it is this range that is at the heart of our book. Although the routes described here are all 'low' mountain walks (**Puig Major**, the island's highest peak, is less than 1500 metres), don't underestimate them. These are serious mountains, the ground is rugged, and one runs all the usual risks of mountain escapades – nobody's going to be complaining the terrain is too tame.

AIM AND SCOPE

The book is aimed at a wide range of walkers, from holidaymakers who want to break the beach-bar-restaurant routine with a leisurely stroll, to dedicated ramblers determined to reach the most remote peaks. For technical reasons, largely to do with mapping and not having something the size of a table cloth wrapping itself round your head in a strong wind, we have limited ourselves to the northern half of the island, but this involves no great sacrifice, as the majority of Mallorca's best walking is to be had in this region. Apart from walks in and around the **Tramuntana**, we also feature some remarkable itineraries in the eastern peninsulas of **Alcúdia** and **Formentor**.

WHEN TO GO

Given the fierce heat of summer, September to May is the ramblers' season. Autumn and Spring are best for birdwatching, April and May for lovers of wild flowers. Winters are generally mild and dry, though snow is not impossible. If you're relying on public transport, schedule your trip for May or September.

THE WALKS

Traditionally many of the classic walking routes in Mallorca are one-way itineraries returning to base by bus or boat, but we have opted for loops on the premise that it's more relaxing to make your own pace and not be hampered by somebody else's timetable - some guidebooks advise readers relying on the bus to 'walk quickly'! Occasionally natural or man-made obstacles oblige us to return by the same route. Classic one-way itineraries are cited and cross-referenced between looped walks.

Timings are all 'pure', excluding snacking, snapping and simply standing still staring. It is highly unlikely you will complete any of these walks in exactly the time specified. Before you tackle the longer routes, time yourself against one of our shorter itineraries, then curse me for a slow-coach or a racing maniac as seems appropriate. Timings marked with a **U** are walks I did 'Unaccompanied', when I tend to walk a little faster. All global timings include the return unless otherwise specified.

The paths are generally well-maintained and waymarked, usually with cairns rather than paint (though you frequently have to know a route exists and commit yourself before finding any waymarks). However, some of the less celebrated routes are neither maintained nor waymarked and some of the itineraries in this book don't follow any paths whatsoever! That said, there are no itineraries detailed here that don't at least have the odd cairn along the way. However, since my routes do not necessarily correspond to the traditional walk, only follow waymarks when they are referred to in the text.

Variation in place names between different publications is terrible. If you're not using our map, beware. Given the complexity of much of the terrain and the impact of human activity, the descriptions are fairly detailed. I've tried to give enough detail for those who need confirmation they're on the right path, but not so much as to irritate more confidant pathfinders with superfluity. For ease of reference, street names at the start of walks are in bold text. *Italics* are used for *discrete Spanish words*, if also in purple, you'll find them explained in the glossary. Consistency rather than deficient vocabulary accounts for all climbs being 'gentle', 'steady', or 'steep'.

PROBLEMS

Violent crime is rare, but petty theft is endemic. <u>Never leave valuables in your car</u>. The most notorious spots are **Cap Formentor**, the **Lluc** monastery car-park and, above all, the parking areas around the **Cúber** reservoir.
Access to private land can be a problem. As a general rule, we've excluded all walks where access is restricted or potentially controversial. If, despite our best efforts, we have chosen a route subsequently closed off, please let us know.

FLORA & FAUNA

Carritx (a word you will see frequently in the descriptions) is the pampas-like diss grass found all over the island. The classic trick with *carritx* is to stand on it with one foot and trip over it with the other. Otherwise, the most common or distinctive flowers and shrubs are Asphodels, Euphorbia (also called spurge), Pistacia (also known as mastic or lentisc), Myrtle, Thyme, Rosemary, Foxglove, Hellebore, Windflowers, Blue Tobacco, and enough orchids to merit a book to themselves. In April the island is awash with brilliant flowering Mimosa, Jacaranda and Judas Trees, but on the whole, the most common trees in the mountains are Pine, Holm Oak, Strawberry Trees, Almond, Oleaster and Olive, the last frequently incredibly ancient and contorted.

Mallorca is a bird watcher's paradise. **The Bóquer Valley** and **S'Albufera** wetlands are world famous, as is the Black Vulture frequently seen in the **Tramuntana**. Other birds to look out for are the Bearded, Griffon and Egyptian Vultures, Booted Eagles, Osprey, Kites, Kestrels, and Falcons (notably the rare Eleanor's Falcon). There are a tremendous number of brightly coloured finches and tits, and more seasonal visitors than I can even begin to catalogue. Thrushes, Swallows, Martins and Partridge are common, and you may also see the wonderfully endearing Hoopoe, with his comical crest and dipping, gravity challenged flight.

As for mammals, reptiles and amphibians, you will occasionally see grandiloquent multilingual notices announcing 'Big Game Hunting'. Don't be deceived. The last big game they had on Mallorca was when the local football team beat Real Madrid and the biggest game most locals get on their plate is a portion of kid culled from the thousands of wild goats that roam the mountains. Wild boar and foxes have long since been wiped out, and the pine marten, genet and feral cats the island boasts might as well have been for all the average rambler sees of them – roadkill for the most part. We saw one weasel, several shrews, and heard loads of toads and frogs, of which the most emblematic is the Mallorcan Midwife Toad. Snakes are rare and not dangerous. Sightings of whales and dolphins are occasionally reported. More details available from the **Lluc Serra Tramuntana** Information Centre.

EATING & DRINKING

It would be entirely possible to spend an entire year on Mallorca without eating anything more alien than bacon and eggs, but assuming you fancy something more adventurous, the following notes might help get you started.

Sopa (soup) *mallorquin* is pretty much a vegetable stew and a good filling meal in itself, while *sopa de matances* and *sopa de pescado* are respectively the meat and fish equivalents. *Allioli* is garlic mayonnaise and *fonoi marí* is pickled sea fennel. *Pa amb oli* is dear to the Mallorca sense of self, but is not that exceptional, just the usual bread and oil found everywhere else in Spain: 'just', I say – it's very good, especially with charcuterie or a few slices of *Mahon*, a salty hard cheese. *Arroz Brut* is the local paella, *tumbat* is a variation on the classic Mediterranean combination of aubergine and tomatoes, and *greixonera* is a casserole. Beef (*ternera*) is a waste of time, but pork (*cerdo* or *porc*) and lamb (*cordero* or *anyell*) are excellent. *Butifarra* or *morcilla* is black-pudding and *sobrasada,* a local speciality, is a kind of *chorizo*-sausage pâté. Sweets and puddings are generally factory-made, but it doesn't matter greatly as the oranges *(naranja*s) are superb. *Zumo de Naranja*, sold everywhere, is fresh orange juice. Where Mallorcans really excel though is at the baker's: *ensaïmada* are light breakfast pastries, often copied elsewhere in Spain, but rarely done as well. *Coca* is the local crumbly-based, vegetable-topped version of pizza (the green topping is a mixture of shard, leek and lashings of parsley) and makes an excellent picnic snack, as do the vegetable pasties (*cocarrois*), and meat and fish pies (*empanada*).

Mallorcan wine can be excellent, notably those from the Binissalem denomination, our favourites being Pere Seda Novell and the wines of Jose L. Ferrer. Hierbas is the local digestive, a herb flavoured anisette.

LANGUAGE

English is spoken in most bars, restaurants and shops, but once you're out in the countryside, it's Spanish, Catalan or pantomime. Everywhere, a few words of Spanish will take you a long way, and a few Catalan phrases even further. Mallorcan Catalan is a less harsh version of the mainland variety, as is the linguistic politics of the islanders, who are not disgruntled if they have to speak Spanish.

ACKNOWLEDGEMENTS

Thanks to IBANAT (the official conservation organisation in the Balearics) for fielding a small army of forestry workers, both professional and voluntary, who not only keep the paths clear and the *áreas recreativas* clean, but are unfailingly courteous and helpful. Special thanks to the staff of the Serra Tramuntana Information Centre at **Lluc**: for expertise, dedication and approachability, they cannot be praised too highly. Special thanks also to Oliver St. John who suggested numerous itineraries, including some that didn't make it into the book because they scared the bejeezus out of me. And, as ever, thanks to Jeannette Tallegas for keeping me fed, watered and approximately clean while I battered away at my keyboard; to Ros and David Brawn for pioneering several of the routes featured here and for helping to solve a surreal succession of technical problems.

SYMBOLS RATING GUIDE

DWG's famous "Symbols Rating Bar' gives you the key information about a walking route in a quick glance. Remember that "Effort/Exertion' and 'Refreshments' are the author's opinion and that 'Time' is the walking time without stops.

  our rating for effort/exertion:-
1 very easy   **2** easy   **3** average
4 energetic   **5** strenuous

  approximate **time** to complete a walk (compare your times against ours early in a walk) - does not include stopping time

  approximate walking **distance** in kilometres

  approximate **ascents/descents** in metres (N = negligible)

  circular route

  linear route

  risk of **vertigo**

  refreshments (may be at start or end of a route only)

Walk descriptions include:
- timing in minutes, shown as (40M)
- compass directions, shown as (NW)
- GPS waypoints, shown as (Wp.3)
- **U** at the start of a walk shows it was done unaccompanied, so generally walked at faster speed

The map sections used in this book have been taken from **Mallorca (North & Mountains) Tour & Trail Map 5th edition** (ISBN 9781904946502)) published by Discovery Walking Guides Ltd in 2009.

All map sections are aligned so that north is at the top of the page. In the interests of clarity adjoining and inter-linking walking routes have been deleted from the map sections for each specific walking route. Waypoint positions, and numbers, refer to the walking route that the map section is illustrating.

ALTITUDE & FEATURES

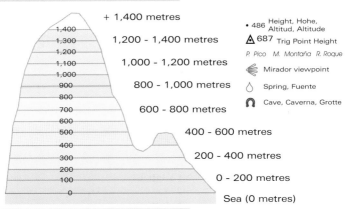

ROADS, TRACKS, TRAILS

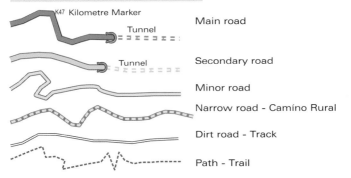

Walking Routes

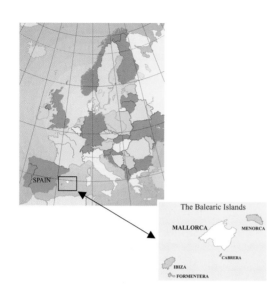

The Balearic Islands

General area covered in the Central Walks section (Walks 9-27)

General area covered in the Western Walks section (Walks 1-8)

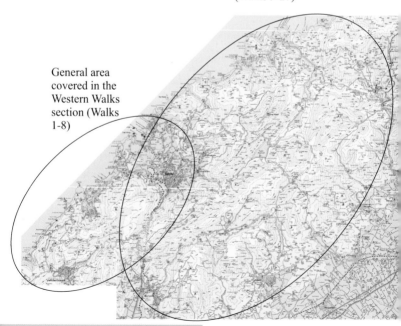

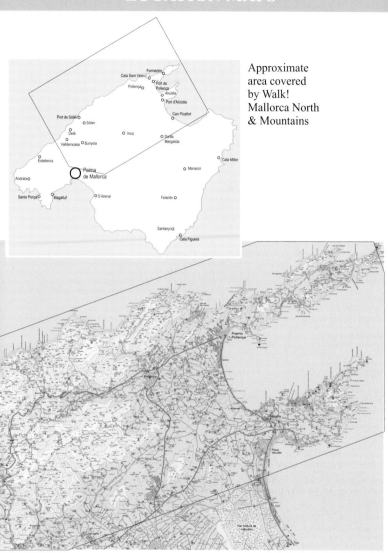

Approximate area covered by Walk! Mallorca North & Mountains

General area covered in the Eastern Walks section (Walks 28-46)

The GPS Waypoint lists provided in this third edition of **Walk! Mallorca (North & Mountains)**, are as recorded by Charles during his research of the walking routes contained in this book. In the interests of clarity, each map section only shows the route and waypoints for that walk. Where a waypoint symbol is shown on a map it has been placed alongside the position to which it refers so as to not obscure the map detail and is numbered so that it can directly identified against the walk description and waypoint list. For readers wondering what we are talking about, GPS Waypoints are also Grid References to the exact locations within each walking route, when used in conjunction with the **Mallorca (North & Mountains) Tour & Trail Map**.

All The GPS Waypoints quoted in Walk! Mallorca (North & Mountains) are subject to the general considerations as to the accuracy of GPS units in the location concerned. Mallorca generally has good GPS reception with little 'mountain shadowing' causing reception problems. One exception is Walk 22, 'Three Pecks at the Torrent de Pareis' where GPS reception is non-existent within the gorge itself, so GPS waypoints are only provided for 22b above the gorge and on 22c for the descent into the gorge until GPS reception becomes unreliable. Walk 6 has poor reception on the descent to Deià, and Walk 16 'Tossals Verds Circuit' has two sections of poor GPS reception in the gorges encountered on the route. Walks 39 & 40 'Creek & Peak' routes have a section of poor reception as we ascend towards the main road. On these routes the lack of GPS reception are on sections of the walk where there is only one logical way and will not compromise your navigational accuracy.

It is almost impossible to reproduce the exact waypoint co-ordinates in practice when walking a route. While waypoints are quoted to 00.0001 minutes of arc, in practice you should expect 10 metres as an acceptable standard of accuracy when you have '3D navigation' (four or more satellites in view); though good reception on Mallorca means that often your accuracy will be closer to 5 metres.

Signal Strength
Signal strength from sufficient satellites is crucial to obtaining an accurate location fix with your GPS unit. In open sky, ridge top, conditions you may have up to 11 satellites in view to give you a GPS location accuracy of 5 metres. Providing you have good batteries, and that you wait until your GPS has full 'satellite acquisition' before starting out, your GPS will perform wonderfully on Mallorca for all our routes, subject to the notes above on routes 16, 22 and 40.

To Input the Waypoints
Waypoint co-ordinates are quoted for the WGS84 datum, used to provide grid references on the Tour & Trail Map, in degrees and minutes of Latitude and Longitude. To input the waypoints into your GPS we suggest that you:
- switch on your GPS and select 'simulator' mode
- check that your GPS is set to the WGS84 datum (its default datum) and the 'location format' 'hddd° .mm.mmm'
- input the GPS waypoints into a 'route' file with the same number as the walking route number; then when you call up the 'route' on Mallorca there will be no confusion as to which walking route it refers to.

- repeat the inputting of routes until you have covered all the routes you plan to walk, or until you have used up the memory capacity of your GPS; most GPS units will store up to 20 routes of up to 50 waypoints for each route, and you can always re-programme your GPS while on Mallorca.
- turn off your GPS. When you turn the GPS back on it should return to its normal navigation mode.

Waypoints are provided as an additional navigation aid to complement the detailed walk descriptions in Walk! Mallorca (North & Mountains). Knowing exactly where you are in relation to our detailed walk description is a great confidence booster when exploring these new and exciting landscapes. GPS Waypoints are provided for all key navigational points on all walking routes; never again should you find yourself wondering whether you are on the right path or not.

Note that GPS Waypoints complement the detailed walking route descriptions in Walk! Mallorca (North & Mountains); and are not intended as an alternative to the detailed walking route description.

Personal Navigator Files (PNFs).
Edited versions of all the GPS tracks and waypoints compiled during Charles Davis' research are available on our **Personal Navigator Files CD.** GPS Utility Special edition software is included on the CD, enabling the user to load track and waypoint information direct to their GPS unit via a PC. In addition to **Mallorca (North & Mountains)** the PNFs CD contains the GPS tracks and waypoints for **Mallorca West**, **Menorca**, **La Gomera**, **La Palma**, **Tenerife**, **Lanzarote**, **Sierra de Aracena**, **Madeira**, **Alpujarras**, **Axarquia**, **Andorra**, and the full **Walk! UK** series of guide books covering **Lake District North**, **Lake District South**, **Yorkshire Dales (North & Central)**, **South Pennines**, **Peak District South**, **Brecon Beacons**, **South Downs**, **Dorset**, **Isle of Wight**, **Devon**, **Dartmoor** and **Exmoor**.

Confused by GPS?

If you are confused by talk of GPS, but are interested in how GPS could enhance your walking enjoyment, then simply seek out a copy of **GPS The Easy Way** (£4.99), the UK's best selling GPS manual. Written in an easy to read, lively, style and lavishly illustrated, GPS The Easy Way takes you through all aspects of GPS usage from absolute basics up to GPS Expert and debunking the myths about GPS along the way; an essential purchase for anyone thinking of buying a GPS.

"A compass points north" but
"A GPS tells you where you are, where you have been, and can show you where you want to go."
"Ask not 'What is GPS?' - ask 'What can GPS do for me?' "

WALKING EQUIPMENT

Walkers are very interested in the clothing and equipment used by other walkers. For some this interest borders on obsession, with heated debates over walking poles, boots versus sandals, GPS versus 'map and compass' navigation etc etc. Walking magazines are packed with clothing and equipment reviews, opinions and adverts, but few walking guide books give more than a cursory mention to recommended clothing and equipment. At the risk of upsetting some walking fundamentalists, here is a brief rundown on what I've used on Mallorca.

Backpack
A 25-30 litre day pack should easily cope with all the equipment you think you will need for a day's walking. A design with plenty of outside pockets to give easy access to frequently used items, such as ½ litre water bottles, is a good starting point. Well padded straps will spread the load and a waist strap will stop the pack moving about on the more adventurous routes. A ventilated back panel will help clear sweat on hot days and tough routes; a design with a stand-off frame is best for ventilation and worth the small increase in weight. Do spend time adjusting the straps so that you get the most comfortable fit.

Footwear
Mallorca's dramatic landscapes offer no compromises, and nor should you compromise on your footwear. While there are many comfortable paths on the island, a lot of the walking is on hard rock, usually uneven. Whether you choose boots, shoes or sandals, they must be up to the task. You will need a hard sole with plenty of grip and a well padded foot-bed. My favourites are a pair of Bestard boots that I picked up at their factory shop on Mallorca. Worn with thick mountain socks, these boots have done everything I have asked of them. (Calzados Bestard, C/. Estación 40-42 Lloseta)

Whichever footwear you choose, do make sure that you have covered plenty of kilometres in them before coming to Mallorca.

Sun Protection
Always carry a comfortable sun hat, also useful should it rain. Choose a design that gives you plenty of shade, is comfortable to wear, and stays on your head in windy conditions. You will be spending several hours a day outdoors and sunburnt ears (and neck) are both painful and embarrassing. Sunglasses and high-factor sun cream are highly recommended.

Water & Food
Always carry as much water as you think you might drink. A couple of ½ litre bottles, a few pence each from local shops, is the minimum, and add another couple of litres for more demanding routes. Even on shorter routes, I would advise that you carry some survival rations. While some routes are well equipped with 'tipico' bars these may not be open when you need them, so survival rations of chocolate bars and the like can provide welcome comfort.

Medical Kit
Antiseptic wipes, antiseptic cream, plasters and bandage are supplemented by lip salve, which can seem like a life saver in hot dry conditions. Also include

tweezers, which you will soon appreciate if you catch a splinter or cactus spine, and a whistle to attract attention if you get into difficulties.

Processionary caterpillars occasionally seen in Pine forests may look cute as they nose-to-tail their way across the trail, but they are a pest, killing trees and causing nasty allergic reactions in some people. If you're prone to allergies, take a supply of antihistimine with you.

Navigation
Do not compromise - buy the best guide book and the best map, and carry them with you. A compass is useful to orientate yourself at the start of a route and for general directions, but a GPS unit is far more useful - see 'Using GPS on Mallorca'.

Clothing
Choose loose comfortable clothing and add a lightweight waterproof jacket to your back pack; the Balearic Islands are famous for sunshine but I saw quite a bit of rain while researching this book.

Other Equipment
You won't want to be carrying excess weight during your walking, especially on the longer routes with major ascents/descents. Digital cameras weigh far less than their film equivalents, and a monocular is half the weight of a pair of binoculars. Secateurs might seem an unusual choice of walking equipment, but they can be useful on some routes. A mobile phone, and money (refreshments, taxis, public telephones, drinks machines etc.) are also recommended.

PRAGMATISTS AND FANTASISTS

Ever since the thirteenth century and the birth of the mystic Ramon Llull, Mallorca has been a land of poets and dreamers, most of whom seem to turn up at the western end of the **Tramuntana**. But professors of otherworldliness rarely exist in isolation and the more romantic visitors to the island have always had to live alongside a profoundly pragmatic people. This combination of lofty ideals and matter-of-fact roots is manifest the minute you arrive in **Valldemossa** from the south.

Crossing the almond dotted plain on the MA-1110, you get the strong impression you're heading for an impenetrable wall of mountain, but after the **Esporles** turning, a breach opens in the **Tramuntana**, and the road winds between olive and pine, climbing to the small valley around **Finca Son Brondo**, from where we get our first glimpse of **Valldemossa** and the western end of the **Teix** massif. A few moments later we see the monastery for which the village is famous. Perched on a pedestal of higgledy-piggledy terraces and surrounded by carefully tailored trees, it's the perfect emblem of Mallorca, a dream in stone, aimed at paradise but raised on decidedly earthy foundations.

Despite the village's development as a daytripper's haven, the impact of arrival probably hasn't changed that much since the Carthusians fell in love with Valldemossa in the fifteenth century and successfully petitioned King Don Martí (described by the Catalan writer and painter Santiago Rusiñol as "a man of such piety, nobody has a word to say about him, either good or bad"!) to give them the remains of the old royal palace.

Admittedly the monastery as it stands today is of relatively recent construction, but this must always have been a spot carefully balanced between heaven and earth, and the work the monks did over the next three centuries only serves to emphasize the dichotomy. When the order was disentailed in the 1830's, its properties throughout Spain were variously sacked by embittered tenants or sold into private hands. Being a practical people, the Mallorcans opted for the latter solution, renting rooms to rich tourists, for whom the simplicity of a monastic cell in the sun was a pleasing antidote to the dark satanic mills of the north.

The most celebrated of the monastery's guests were George Sand and Frederic Chopin, who visited Mallorca in 1838, hoping the island climate would improve Chopin's health. As it happened, an unusually dismal winter did more damage than good, a disappointment expressed in Sand's rather dyspeptic account of their season on the island, 'A Winter In Majorca'. To make matters worse, the Mallorcan peasant proved altogether too down-to-earth for the romantic nineteenth century imagination, resulting in some quite rancorous comments about the islanders. But the pragmatic nature that disappointed Sand has ensured her local immortality, and 'A Winter In Majorca' is now sold everywhere in every language.

Happier results came of the spot of bad weather encountered by the Archduke

Ludwig Salvador, a member of the Austrian royal family who preferred messing about in the Mediterranean to observing the more decorous rites of Viennese court life. Stuck in a rainstorm, the Archduke decided the only sane response was to buy a house, which he duly did, with the simple injunction that the owner, Señor Serra, name his price and make it fair as Ludwig wasn't a man to haggle and would only say yes or no. Being a pragmatic Mallorcan, Señor Serra named a fair price, so pleasing the Archduke he carried on buying farms for the next forty years, turning himself in the process into a one-man Mallorcan heritage industry.

Heading east from **Valldemossa**, we soon pass the first of the Archduke's purchases, **Miramar**. Loosely translated, miramar means 'Sea View', a name deceptively suggestive of a Sussex bungalow. As sea-views go though, **Miramar** is of a different order to anything found in England. Here the sea is so expansive and so invasive, reports from the 1930's suggest certain old men among the local population believed the island actually floated on the water, detached from any more solid mooring. And if testimony is required concerning the sea's colour, a deep, shifting camouflage of azure mottled indigo, one need only recall the story of a small boy who wouldn't go swimming because he feared turning blue.

After **Miramar**, the landscape opens out, the tightly packed pine and holm oak woods giving way to more spacious olive groves as we approach **Son Marroig** (another of the Archduke's country pads), beyond which **Puig Major**, the island's highest summit, and the rocky coast between **Deià** and **Sóller** come into view. Clustered round a small knoll tucked between the **Teix** massif and the sea, **Deià** has been located with considerable care, near enough to the exquisite little **Cala de Deià** for the purposes of communicating with the outside world, but far enough from the coast to have warning of marauding pirates.

In this instance, pragmatism played a hand that appealed to the romantics, too, and the village has attracted numerous artists and writers, notably the poet, novelist and mythologist, Robert Graves. Although the romance Graves espoused was of a different order to George Sand's, it was romance nonetheless, and it's no accident that a man who once went climbing with Mallory should end his days in **Deià**. There are several classic 'walks' here that I decided not include since they seemed closer to cliff face escapades than conventional rambling. **Deià** is now a popular tourist destination better known for its business magnates than its poets and can hardly be called the epitome of romance, but it's still visually stunning and remains sufficiently atmospheric to have one yearning for superficially less complicated times and the 'simple' life celebrated by more than one generation of romantic thinkers.

Leaving **Deià**, the narrow road curls along the contour line flanked by immaculately maintained terraces; and woe betide anyone in a hurry who happens to get stuck behind a bus and a pack of cyclists - overtaking is strictly for the suicidal and homicidal. Passing between **Can Prohom** and **Son Bleda**, we come to the western limit of our central section, the **Sóller** plain, home to the last, most local and most numerous of our fantasists.

Quiz show question: what's the world capital of oranges?
a. Seville   b. Valencia   c. Israel   d. Sóller

Most people would probably choose one of the first three options - unless they've already visited **Sóller**. The name comes from the Arabic for 'a golden shell', a suitably evocative description to give you an idea of this fertile valley, home to scores of small orange groves, the fruit of which has to be tasted rather than described. These oranges were the desideratum for the migrant dreamers of the **Sóller** diaspora, the adventurers that spread around the world in the nineteenth and twentieth centuries, working abroad for ten, twenty, forty years, however long it took to get the money to buy a patch of land at home and cultivate their garden. And all the while, they dreamed of the oranges they would grow, oranges so succulent and sweet, they remained bright in the mind's eye throughout forty years of wandering. It was a very Mallorcan dream, going away to get closer to home, seeing the world in order to settle on native soil - perhaps a pragmatist's fantasy!

WESTERN WALKS LOCATOR MAP

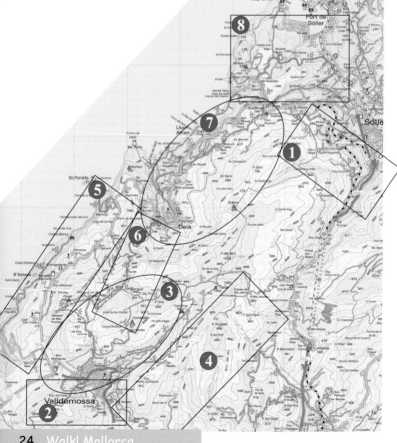

1 CAMÍ DE CASTELLO

This variation on the classic climb from **Sóller** to **Can Prohom** is an ideal introduction to walking in Mallorca. Following country lanes, cobbled donkey trails, dirt tracks and clear paths, it's easy walking all the way, winding between typically well-maintained terraces dotted with modest cabins and the occasional magisterial country home. Frequent shady passages mean this is a practical itinerary on a hot day, and a dense fringe of wild gladioli will reward flower-lovers in spring. Revising this itinerary for the new edition, we re-walked the start until Wp.9, where the new signposting that appears at all subsequent junctions begins, then descended via the **Camí de Rocafort**, a lovely cobbled trail that I highly recommend for a shorter walk snaking down to the by-pass in a little under a kilometre.

* + 20 minutes return to **Can Prohom**

Extension	Stroll
Turn left at Wp.12. Follow the dirt track for 50 metres then take the broad path skirting the field, arriving at the chapel just below **Can Prohom** (10M from Wp.12). See Walks 7 & 8 for longer excursions from this point.	Take the bus to **Can Prohom** for the descent back to **Sóller**
	Short Versions
	See text

Access: on foot from **Sóller**.

From the **Plaza d'Espanya** in **Sóller**, where the tourism office is, we take **Carrer de Isabel II** (Wp.1 0M) and follow it till it ends 550 metres later at the southernmost roundabout on the by-pass, where we maintain direction (N) up the MA-11 for another 50-metres, then cross onto the narrow concrete lane immediately to the left of House No.6 (Wp.2 8M).

Forking left twice in the first 100 metres (Wps. 3 & 4), we climb steeply, carrying straight on (the right hand branch) when we run into a U-bend (Wp.5 13M), after which the gradient eases off. We soon put the racket of the by-pass behind us as the lane winds through immaculately maintained terraces of olive and carob trees. Veering right at a junction with a cobbled trail (Wp.6 31M), we stay on the lane to cross the **Palma-Sóller** railway line 100 metres later.

The dwindling end of the surfaced lane curves away to the left in front of a house with a large, arched gate and a weather-beaten sign on the wall for 'Camino de Casteo por s'Heretat y Can Prohom', at which point we carry straight on along a dirt track (Wp.7 38M), that becomes a path a little under 300 metres later. A lovely, shady stroll below overhanging oak leads to a triple fork, where we ignore the gated branches on the left and descend to the right (Wp.8 48M) to the signposted junction with the **Camí de Rocafort** (Wp.9 51M) where we turn right for a shorter walk or carry straight on for the main walk, soon reaching a stretch where the old *camí* has been widened to a dirt track.

the track after Wp.7

After a gentle descent,
we climb behind a recently restored house, where we find a stretch of concrete and a waypost indicating we leave the track to recover the original narrow path (Wp.10 56M).

The path climbs steps crossing the **Cinc Ponts Torrent**, beyond which we cross a wayposted junction of dirt tracks. Maintaining direction (NW), we climb steeply on a rough concrete track, recovering the path 30 metres later at another waypost and painted rock sign in front of **Can Paies**. The path tunnels through a dense overgrowth of pistacia then continues through successive stretches of shade and sun, level and descent, before going through a rough wire gate. Strolling along immaculate terraces, we approach a large house fronted by a tall palm tree, just before which we come to our second shortcut option, a signposted path on the right, **Camí des Monts Reals** (Wp.11 66M).

To continue on the **Camí de Castello**, we go through the gated courtyard behind the large house, taking care to shut both gates behind us, after which a steady climb along a cobbled donkey trail brings us through another rough gate onto a dirt track between a small cabin and a stand of pine on a knoll topped with a gazebo. We bear right on the dirt track to maintain direction (NW), already in sight of **La Muleta** (see Walk 8). The track becomes a tarmac lane passing behind the luxurious **Cas Xorc Hotel**, at the gates of which (Wp.12 81M) we have a choice, turning left to continue along the **Camí de Castello** to **Can Prohom** and the longer extensions, or right to descend to **Sóller**.

Turning right for **Sóller**, we follow the wayposted dirt track, the **Camí des Rost**, past a first branch on the left (ending in a pleasant picnic spot if desired). The track then climbs towards a gate, just before which we bear left on a wayposted path (Wp.13 91M). After going through a rough gate, we join a cobbled path that soon broadens to a stepped donkey trail. Following a 100 metre stretch thinly coated with tarmac, we recover the cobbled trail which descends steeply to the junction with the **Camí des Monts Real** (see Wp.11). The cobbles eventually run into a tarmac lane, passing the junction for **Camí de Rocafort** (see Wp.9), 50 metres after which we bear left at House Nº1 to rejoin the **Sóller** by-pass in front of the petrol station (115M). For the town centre, take the lane to the right of the petrol station.

Replacing such an exceptional walk as the climb to **Teix** from **Coll de Sóller** after it was fenced off was no easy matter, especially since several options I dreamed up were in turn curtailed by *Prohibido el Paso* signs or landowners who were less than delighted to see my cheery face on their property. Eventually, we opted for a brief but strenuous climb onto the **Sa Comuna** ridge to the west of **Valldemossa**, from where we have superb views of the **Teix** massif, the **Molas de Son Ferrandell** and **Son Pacs**, and the wide expanse of the azure blue sea, not only to the north, but to the south, too. For the most part, the walk follows the **GR221**, though you wouldn't know it from the waymarking, the sum total of GR insignia being a solitary and rather forlorn signpost planted in the middle of nowhere. So much the better, perhaps, for while the eastern routes out of **Valldemossa** are so well known they can get a little crowded, the **Sa Comuna** ridge is largely and unjustly neglected. The day we were up there, we had the place to ourselves.

4 | 1½ H | 4 km | 300m / 300m | ⟷ | 4 *

* in Valldemossa **Stroll**:- Molide sa Beata

Our itinerary starts at the northern end of **Valldemossa**, just opposite the bus stop and large coachpark where the 'MA1110' becomes the 'MA1130' (Wp.1 0M).

We take **Carrer de Uruguay** toward the **Reial Cartuja**, turning right 30 metres later between houses Nºs1 & 2 to head toward the distinctive turret of the **Es Molinet** windmill, now a private house. Immediately behind the mill, tucked into a small parking bay (Wp.2 3M), we take a narrow path climbing onto the northern flank of the **Moli de sa Beata**, a wooded hill topped with the eponymous mill.

Es Molinet

A gentle climb brings us to a junction with a stepped path climbing left to the top of the *moli*, but we fork right twice (Wp.3 8M) to reach the corner of a house and a gateway into the **Font de na Llambies** (Wp.4 9M). Going through the gateway, we climb behind the house along a partially cobbled trail.

the trail after Wp.4

After climbing steadily then steeply alongside a boundary wall, we go

Valldemosa seen after Wp.4

through a waymarked gap in another wall to reach a glade where there is a ruin, a covered cistern and the solitary GR waypost (Wp.5 22M).

The path splits into two forks here. For the present, we leave the main trail and take the left fork climbing in a southerly direction. 150 metres later, we ignore a faint path off to the left and cross the principal boundary wall via stone steps set in the wall (Wp.6 26M). Strolling through the woods, we soon rejoin the main trail beside another cistern (Wp.7 29M), where we turn left to climb onto the main ridge.

Waypoint 6

Once on the top, where you turn back is a matter of taste as the various vantage points (south to **Palma**, the plain, and the port, north to the great expanse of blue beyond **Port de Valldemossa**, east to **Teix**, and west to the molas) are all equally attractive. To reach the highest point along the ridge, we stick with the main path as it winds through the woods until it crosses a broken wall beside a roofed corral. 50 metres after passing a second roofed corral, the path starts to descend more steeply, at which point we fork right (Wp.8 39M) and climb across bare rock to reach an unmarked rocky outcrop (Wp.9) take care though as there's a nasty little drop on the far side.

We return the same way with the options of staying on the main trail at Wp.7 to reach Wp.5 via a gate in the wall, and turning right at Wp.4 to circle the **Moli de sa Beata**.

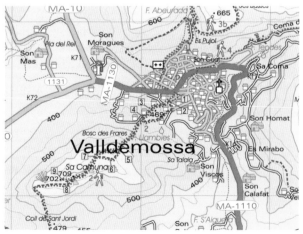

3 THE ARCHDUKE'S PATH from VALLDEMOSSA

In 1867 the Austrian Archduke Ludwig Salvator visited Mallorca and liked it so much he stayed, establishing a tradition that has continued unabated to the present day. Ludwig, however, was more ambitious than modern migrants. His season in the sun was conceived on a large scale and, rather than settling for a modest villa by the sea, he instigated a series of grandiose building projects, among them **Son Moragues** in **Valldemossa**, **Son Marroig** (see Walk 5b), and **S'Estaca** (see Walk 5a), the current retreat of Michael Douglas. Nor was Ludwig a man to take his rustic pleasures lightly. Instead of toiling along charcoal-burners' paths, he set about improving the **Teix** massif, laying a bridleway complete with refuges and *miradors*, a rich man's folly for which generations of walkers have been grateful. Parts of the path are a little too vertiginous for some tastes, but in this itinerary we visit the lower, less alarming stretch. Easy walking, ideal for a family excursion.

We describe two alternative loops: A: **Mirador de ses Puntes**, and B: via **Fontanelles**

A: MIRADOR DE SES PUNTES

					400m			
3	2H	*	7 km					0
					400m			

* + 10 minutes if walking from the town centre to Wp.1

Extension	Stroll
Numerous possibilities, linking with Part B for a larger loop, Walk 4 to climb **Teix**, or Walk 6 to traverse the massif and descend to **Deià**.	100 metres after the stile, bear left over a line of stones to pass a dry spring and stroll along the wooded terrace above **Valldemossa**. Return the same way.
Short Version: To **Es Pouet**	

Access: on foot from **Valldemossa** (accessible by bus from **Palma** & **Sóller**).

From the fountain car-park on the main drag through **Valldemossa**, we take **Carrer de la Venerable Sor Aina** towards the cemetery and football pitch, then second right onto **Carrer de Joan Fuster**, and first left onto **Carrer de les Oliveres**. If arriving by car, park at the end of this road.

The first ladder stile

From the **Oliveres** turning circle we take the gated dirt track (Wp.1 0M) for 150 metres until it is cut by a fence, where we turn left on a broad trail up to a wooden gate and ladder stile. Ignoring waymarked shortcuts immediately after the stile and after 20M, we follow the main trail as it climbs steadily through the wood to go through a wall gateway (Wp.2 30M) into the flat **Pla d'es Pouet**.

Carrying straight on through the woods for 200 metres brings us to the **Es**

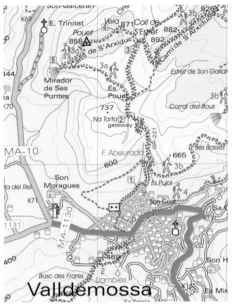

Pouet well, where we bear right on a broad trail (NE). After a pleasant stroll through the peaceful woods we climb, gently then steadily, to the **Coll de s'Estret de son Gallard**, where we join the **Archduke's Path** (Wp.3 45M). Turning left, we soon come into fine views of the cliffs below the higher part of the bridleway. Continuing our climb, we see in succession the sea, the headland at **Port de Sóller**, and **Puig Major** and **Massanella**, before coming to the roofless refuge on **Puig Veia** (Wp.4 60M).

Following the cobbled bridleway, we pass the **Pover** trig point and a natural *mirador* overlooking the coast before descending to the decaying ramparts of the **Mirador de ses Puntes** (Wp.5 75M) where there are tremendous views across the **Valldemossa** plain towards **Galatzó** and, predictably enough, an equally tremendous drop. Five metres behind the *mirador*, the bridleway bears east for a gentle, shady stroll back to the well (90M), a little over thirty minutes from the start.

B: via FONTANELLES

We split the **Archduke's Path** into two because some people find the higher stretch a little vertiginous. To be honest, you'd have to suffer pretty acute vertigo to be disturbed by the drops here, which only inspired a mild toe-tingling in me: the cliffs are high, but the path is well made and flanked to the south by a gentle slope. As it happens though, pragmatic considerations have resulted in two walks we found more satisfying done separately than as a single itinerary. Better still, this gave us the opportunity to include the little known ascent via **Fontanelles**, a delightful climb that avoids queuing behind the large hiking parties ploughing up the traditional route. Apart from a few cognoscenti like Oliver St. John, who suggested this route, the only people you're likely to meet on this ascent are Mallorcans.

* + 40 minutes return for the short extension to Wp.5

Stroll	Extension
to the first *sitjes* between Wps.1&2.	Turn right at Wp.4 for the **Teix** (see text), right after Wp.6 for **Deià**, or carry straight on at Wp.8 for the **Mirador de ses Puntes**.

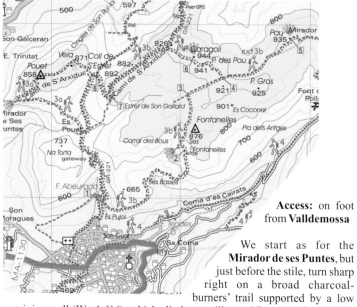

Access: on foot from **Valldemossa**

We start as for the **Mirador de ses Puntes**, but just before the stile, turn sharp right on a broad charcoal-burners' trail supported by a low retaining wall (Wp.1 5M), which climbs steadily, rapidly rewarding us with fine views of **Valldemossa**. After 15M the path levels out and goes through a wall gateway, from where it winds round a broad wooded valley. It then climbs again, becoming a little overgrown, before swinging left at a distinctive, triple-trunked pine for a final climb, varying from steep to steady, ending at a *sitja* and ruined shelter (Wp.2 45M).

Just behind the *sitja* in the trees to your right, you may notice a small cairn. If so, ignore it! This is one of the demented shortcuts impatient Mallorcans pioneer to confuse foreigners. Instead, we maintain direction (NW), leaving the *sitja* on our right. 10 metres later, cairns and old red waymarks indicate our way over the rocks onto an oak-wooded ridge. On our left 100 metres later, there's a fine natural *mirador* on rocks clustered round a large pine. Returning to the wooded ridge, we follow the cairns (NE), climbing over two outcrops of rock to emerge on the rough limestone plateau below **Fontanelles**; we don't actually climb to its summit, which is in any case hard to distinguish among a myriad of competing small tops, but follow the cairn-marked way through the rocks and asphodels (NNE). Bearing NNW as we come onto the larger rocks and still following the cairns (carefully as there is no other clear orientation point), we cross the plateau to join a branch of the **Archduke's Path** (Wp.3 60M) (NOTE: this path isn't normally classified as part of the Archduke's Bridleway, but that's what the locals call it and it was obviously laid at about the same time). Bearing right, we climb a gentle slope to join the main **Archduke's Path** (Wp.4 70M) next to a small stand of pine, at the heart of which is a small shelter built around the roots of a fallen tree.

Extension

For a short extension and/or to climb **Teix**, turn right and follow the 'motorway' (hopefully avoiding traffic jams) as it crosses a shallow depression before climbing to two small tops overlooking **Cala de Deià** and **Sa Foradada** (Wp.5 10M [from Wp.4] the second top). Continuing on the path for ten minutes as it zigzags down beyond the tops brings us to the junction with the path up to **Teix** (Wp.20 of Walk 4).

For the main walk

We turn left at Wp.4 and climb past a first small top to a knoll with a short access path, **Puig Caragoli** (Wp.6, 75M). A couple of minutes later, the **Archduke's Path** passes the cairn-marked descent to **Deià** (see Walk 6), after which we reach its 'vertiginous' stretch (a mere toe-tingler, I assure you) along the clifftops. The views are magnificent, most notably of **Sa Foradada** (see Walk 5). When the path starts zigzagging down through the pine trees, look for a branch to the right after about five minutes of descent, signposted with a small wooden panel suspended from the trees (Wp.7 110M), where we leave the main path and descend through the oak wood to the **Coll de s'Estret** and its V-shaped bench (Wp.8 120M [Wp.3 of alternative loop A]). To continue along the **Archduke's Path**, carry straight on (see above). Otherwise, bear left and follow the broad trail down through the wood to reach **Es Pouet** well in ten minutes. Bear left (S) to cross the *pla* and go through the wall gateway onto the red-waymarked trail back to our starting point in a little under thirty minutes.

Nobody ever complained about the original version of this itinerary, which was conceived with the express intention of getting off the beaten track, well off, yet still reaching the summit of what must be one of Mallorca's most popular mountains. Nonetheless, given its Extreme Path Finding, I felt it was only fair to repeat the **Serra Cairats** ascent for the third edition of this book to see if there had been any changes. There have! The waymarks that inspired the previous version have given up the faint ghost they retained and gone AWOL. Fortunately, there is now an easier but no less spectacular cairn-marked alternative that's so very good, I can recommend repeating the itinerary, even if you only do the short version, which would do very nicely for an early morning walk on a hot day. If you're new to walking in **Mallorca**, all I can say is that this is a must-do.

N.B. The **Serra des Cairats** is called **Serra de Son Moragues** on some maps.

Short Version: turn left at Wp.16 to rejoin the main route at Wp.21. 2h30, same exertion rating.

To reach the start on foot: from the playground at the eastern end of **Valldemossa**, follow the MA1110 toward **Palma** for 100 metres then climb the stairs on the left just before the bottle bank. Turn right to pass the house with the castellated tower and follow **Carrer Lluis Vives** into **Carrer Xesc Forteza**. 100 metres after a carob tree on an island in the road, bear left on a narrow dirt track signposted '*Refugi*' (Wp.1 0M).

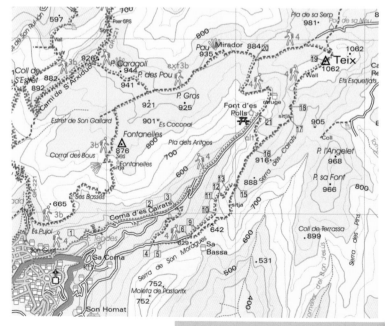

To reach the start by car: follow the MA1110 toward **Palma** then take the first turning on the left, signposted 'Urbanizacion s'Arxiduc/Refugi Son Moragues'. The urbanizacion road climbs to the left to pass a large house (no.20) with imposing black gates. The walk starts on the track (Wp.1 0M) branching off to the right just before this house.

200 metres from the road, the track goes through new gates. We stay on the main track for a little over a kilometre, ignoring minor branches to left and right accessing terraces. After a second new gate and a cattle grid, we bear left into the **Cairats Valley** (Wp.2 15M). 200 metres later, we leave the main track and double back to the right on a minor track zigzagging up in a southwesterly direction (Wp.3 19M).

Ignoring a minor divergence to the right, we climb to a T-junction (Wp.4 30M), where we turn left then fork right 50 metres later (Wp.5) on a cairn-marked shortcut across a bend in the track. After we rejoin it, the track dwindles to a trail shadowing a terracing wall, at the end of which it divides into two narrow paths (Wp.6 41M). We take the cairn-marked path climbing to the right, then turn left at a T-junction 25 metres later (Wp.7).

50 metres after that, we reach a fork, which is where the new version of this ascent diverges from the old. Taking the left hand fork (Wp.8), we pass a *sitja* after another 50 metres. We then cross a second sitja (Wp.9) and bear right, following the path as it traverses the slope, passing a metal 'Ca a Controlada' sign (Wp.10 52M).

Keeping an eye out for successive cairns, we cross two distinct bands of rock, beyond which we reach the foot of a steep, gully-like pass (Wp.11 56M). A brief but strenuous scramble, occasionally hands on and generally ankle deep in leaf mulch (beware of dislodging loose stones if there are other people behind you), brings us to the top of the pass where

the pass

descending to the font - short version

there is a third *sitja* (Wp.12 63M). Our path then climbs through the rocks to the right, fine views opening out over **Valldemossa** and the mountains to the west. The path levels off as it approaches concentric sitjes (Wp.13 69M), after which a cairn up to our right (Wp.14) indicates a way through the rocks to reach twin *sitjes*, above which we join the broad trail used in the previous version of this itinerary (Wp.15 74M).

Turning left, we take a well-earned breather as we stroll along the broad trail to join the **Serra Cairats** trail (AKA **Cami des Caragol**) at a U-bend (Wp.16 81M). For the short version rejoining the main track at **Font des Polls**, turn left to enjoy an easy descent along a lovely snaking trail that reaches Wp.21 in a little over 10 minutes.

For **Teix**, turn right, climbing steadily until the trail ends at the last *sitja* (Wp.17 96M), where a rough stony way dotted with cairns and red waymarks climbs (E) to a wall topped with a fence. Bearing left, we follow the wall for 50 metres before crossing it by a second waymarked breach (Wp.18 112M). Thereafter, frequent cairns and waymarks guide us up a steep, but relatively easy climb across the rocks (NE) to a gap in the wall girdling the southern side of the **Teix**, from where a gentler climb leads to the trig point on the summit (Wp.19 132M).

To return to the **Cairats Valley**, we descend (ENE) to the coll between **Teix** and its sister peak, where we bear left (NNW) down to the **Pla de sa Serp** plateau. Following the broad, obvious trail (WNW) we cross a slight rise to a Y-junction just before a wall. The two branches rejoin beyond the wall for a final rocky descent to a large pile of stones on the **Archduke's Path** (Wp.20 147M).

limekiln in the Cairats valley

Bearing left, we follow a wellstabilized path zigzagging down to the **Son Moragues** refuge, where the broad dirt track descending into the **Cairats Valley** begins. 200 metres later, we come to the **Font des Polls** picnic area, where the short version joins the main itinerary from the left (Wp.21 172M).

From here, we simply follow the track down, down, down to return to the start, a descent that is very straightforward and initially very hard on the knees until the gradient eases and we leave the **Son Moragues Area Recreativa** via a stone-stepped stile. 200 metres after the stile, a waymarked shortcut slices across a final S-bend just short of Wp.3.

5 SA FORADADA

A: THE LOST PATH

Sa Foradada is the classic picture-postcard peninsula between **Deià and Valldemossa**. For many years this attractive coastal route was dubbed the **Camí Perdúa** or 'Lost Path' after half of it fell into the sea. If you do the whole thing you may conclude it's still lost as the exhausting rock-hopping route pioneered by local ramblers couldn't be called a 'path' even by the most panglossian hiker. But the first half is very easy, an ideal family excursion, and the second half is at once a geologist's dream and a happy regression to childhood for those who have fond memories of messing about on rocky beaches when they were kids.

* Full version 4, Short Versions (a) 2 (b) 1
** + 20 minutes for the extension
  Short Versions (a) 1¼ hours return, (b) 1½ hours return
*** At the **Sa Foradada** bar - if it's open

Short Version	Stroll
(a) to **Cala S'Estaca** (b) to Wp.5	To **S'Estaca** house and back
Version (a) is the more attractive option, but the steep descent (and re-ascent!) and deep waters at **S'Estaca** mean (b) is preferable for families, even though it's longer. If bathing at **Codols-Blancs**, 'jellies' or plastic sandals are advisable.	**Extension** To **Cala S'Estaca**. Groups with two cars could combine (a) & (b) to avoid doing the 'lost' bit both ways.

Access: by car. Take the MA-1131 to **Port de Valldemossa**. There's room for one large or two small cars just before and again just after km3.6. At a pinch, there's a parking space for one small car at the next sharp bend.

To start, we go down the road and turn right, just before km4, onto the **Sa Marina/Font Figuera** concrete track (Wp.1 0M). The track passes three houses and two gates, the second of which may be shut but can be passed by a pedestrian gate to the left (Wp.2 15M). Shortly after the second gate, we ignore a waymarked path descending to the left and continue on the concrete, soon coming into view of the white towers of the **S'Estaca** house, built by the Archduke Ludwig Salvator and now owned by the film star Michael Douglas. (N.B. This is not the extension!)

After climbing behind the well-tended vineyards of **S'Estaca** (it's a wonder the man has time to make any films) we start descending, ignoring a cairn-marked path climbing to the right, and getting our first sight of the **Sa Foradada** peninsula. When the concrete track bears sharp left between two pillars (Wp.3 30M), usually chained off, we take the dirt track branching right.

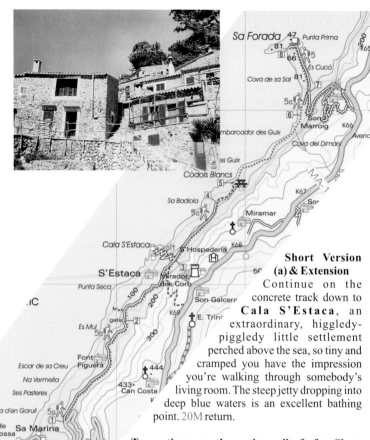

Continue on the concrete track down to **Cala S'Estaca**, an extraordinary, higgledy-piggledy little settlement perched above the sea, so tiny and cramped you have the impression you're walking through somebody's living room. The steep jetty dropping into deep blue waters is an excellent bathing point. 20M return.

To continue on the main walk & for Short Version (b)

We stroll down the shady dirt track to cross a ladder stile (Wp.4 40M), after which the track dwindles to a path. The path descends to a *sitja*, where it doubles back to the left (NW) to a large rock with red-painted requests not to leave litter (Wp.5 50M). Just behind this rock is an idyllic picnic spot with benches and a table. The onward route isn't very long but it is exhausting and every step of the way is a potential disaster: don't continue in trainers unless you've got elephant ankles. My two companions wisely chose to stay on the stony **Codols-Blancs** beach. But for those of you who are happy hopping from rock to rock…

To continue on the lost path

We bear right, as indicated by red arrows, to pass the ruins of a cabin. Ignoring the clear path branching right from the cabin, we bear left to descend steeply past a fallen pine down to a cairn. We then pick our way across the rocks and descend onto the stony **Codols-Blancs** *cala*.

What follows is no harder than crossing the *cala*, but it is remorseless and you'll end up drenched with sweat. A couple more cairns lead us out of the *cala*, after which it's essentially a question of more of the same, scrambling over the larger rocks, hopping over the smaller, dabbing the sweat from your eyes and looking out for those ankles.

You can't get lost as **Sa Foradada** is directly in front of you, but when the way isn't obvious, look for the cairns indicating the easiest route. And do stop once in a while. One can be so busy watching one's feet, it's easy to forget the huge 'eye' at the tip of **Sa Foradada** ('drilled' or 'pierced') which gradually comes into view. After a good, or possibly not so good, fifty minutes of hopping along the rocks, we recover the old path (Wp.6 100M), either passing under a fallen pine to climb directly onto the path (not obvious) or scrambling up a slope to a cairn 30 metres later. The path widens almost immediately to a trail that joins the main track down from **Son Marroig** (Wp.7 105M) where we bear left and stroll along to the neck of the peninsula (Wp.8 115M [see Wp.3 of the **Son Marroig** descent]). Returning by the same route takes about 1½ hours excluding the extension (don't ask why, but it was quicker uphill!).

B: FROM SON MARROIG

Son Marroig is another of the Archduke Ludwig's country pads and can be visited as part of this easy walk for those who don't fancy the gymnastics of The Lost Path. An ideal walk for a misty morning when nobody else is about and the mountains are under cloud. Some books say you need to ask permission to go down (confirmed by notices at the start) others that permission is implicit in purchasing a ticket to visit the house. We couldn't find anyone interested in giving us permission and the bar-keeper said we didn't need it.

Access: by car or bus (km 65.5 MA-10)

From the main doors of **Son Marroig** (Wp.1 0M), we walk up the tarmac lane (SE) past the lion-head fountain and, 50 metres later, climb over the ladder-stile at the green 'No-pasa-sin autorizacion' gate. Following the initially concreted track on the other side of the gate, we bear right at the Y-junction a couple of hundred metres later.

The stony track winds down past superb cliffs that look like they're melting, passing yet another *mirador* constructed by the Archduke, a man for whom a good view was never enough, before it is joined by the track leading to The Lost Path (Wp.2 35M). After strolling along to the neck of the peninsula (Wp.3 45M), we have a choice between a swim from the **Playola** jetty, a drink in the bar (rarely open before midday), or (not recommended since only climbers can descend to the hole) a scramble onto the **Foradada** rock itself. We return by the same route (85M).

This complicated ascent from the **Hotel es Molí** is not well known and rarely appears on maps, let alone in guidebooks, which is baffling because it's a superb route, while the descent along the **Caragoli Camí des Cingles** is, metre for metre, probably the most spectacular path on the entire island. I can only suppose the pathfinding difficulties on the way up and the apparent impossibility from afar of the descent have discouraged previous researchers. Fortunately, locals have been more tenacious and the charcoal burners' paths we use on this itinerary have been kept opened and marked (to a greater or lesser degree) with cairns. This is another suggestion for which we have to thank Oliver St. John. The descent should not be undertaken when visibility is poor and I recommend gaining some familiarity with the **Archduke's Path** on one of the easier ascents from **Valldemossa** before tackling this itinerary.

N.B. There may be hunters at weekends in the hunting season in the next estate; you might see their hides from above **Son Rullan** around waypoint 8.

Stroll	Extension
- to Wp.4	See Walks 3 & 4 for **Teix** and/or traverses to **Valldemossa**

Access: on foot from **Hotel Es Molí** at the western limit of **Deià**. Ask permission to use the hotel car-park.

Overlooking Hotel Es Molí

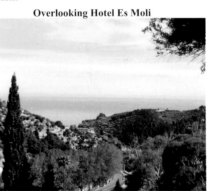

From the top of the hotel car-park (Wp.1 0M), we climb the tarmac lane behind the hotel, passing above the swimming pool and winding through two hairpin bends, after which the tarmac gives way to a dirt track.

Ignoring a concrete branch on the left, we continue along the dirt track towards a farmhouse, 50 metres before which, we bear left on a cobbled path marked with a hand-made sign for 'Es Teix / Valldemossa' (Wp.2 10M).

The path, which switches between cobbles and dirt and is sometimes overgrown with *carritx*, was part of the network giving access to the abandoned terraces behind **Hotel Es Molí** and can be confusing due to branches onto individual terraces. There are at least two cairn-marked routes across the terraces, so don't worry if you see cairns off your path. Just follow the right bank (our left) of the small valley (SW), looking for cairns every 50-75 metres.

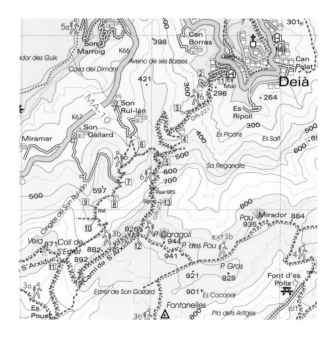

Climbing steadily across the terraces, we ignore a wall gateway onto the valley's left bank and continue climbing for another 100 metres to go through a second wall gateway (Wp.3 25M). Take care a couple of minutes after this gateway to turn sharp right, away from the apparently clearer route across a bare sloping rock, to maintain a general SSW direction, passing under the natural arch of a splintered pine.

At a small cabin (Wp.4 40M) fronted by a small trough carved into the rock, we bear right onto the northern side of the valley, either passing below or above (the two paths rejoin) a dry tunnelled spring

Fifty metres after the two paths rejoin, we bear left on another cobbled section leading to a cascade of terraces. After 30 metres, the cobbled path rejoins a dirt and stone path, and we bear left to go through a long, lazy, shallow zigzag. Bearing left again, away from rusty metal gates, we follow a level track, which soon climbs gently into the oak forest.

Ignoring a major branch to the left, we continue climbing and, 75 metres later, bear sharp right, passing a small red waymark to climb steadily to a first *sitja*. Bearing right again, we climb past another, larger carved trough (there were some <u>very</u> patient people living up here), 30 metres after which the main path swings left.

We leave the main path here, bearing right onto a second *sitja*, just beyond which there's a small bread oven (Wp.5 60M). This is an important junction. Sensible, linear-minded people will turn sharp left immediately after the bread oven and follow the cairn-marked route up to **Puig Caragoli**. The rest of you can follow me!

Crossing a line of stones and branches intended to prevent precisely this sort of thing happening, we maintain direction (W) on a clear, level path that soon dips down and bears left (SW) to a gap in a fence/wall flanked with a lime-kiln and an octagonal carved stone basin (Wp.6 65M). Ignoring the track through the gap in the wall, we bear left, staying on the near side of the fence/wall, bringing the superb **Son Rullan** farmhouse into view. Fifty metres later, we go through a gate in a lateral fence and descend two large natural rock steps. Passing another carved trough, we continue alongside the main fence/wall for 100 metres to a large *sitja* at the end of a dirt track, which, 50 metres later, joins a larger stony track climbing from **Son Rullan**.

Bearing left, we follow this track up through two hairpin bends until it levels off at the remains of another large *sitja*. Cairns on our left indicate a way up through the trees, but it's easier to continue on the track, passing a small bread oven, 40 metres after which, as the track bears right, we turn left onto a charcoal burners' trail (Wp.7 75M). The trail climbs steadily, passing *sitjes* and the very occasional cairn, before virtually disappearing at a final *sitja* and ruined shelter (Wp.8 85M).

Cairns just above the *sitja* lead us onto a faint trail that climbs to cross and recross an old wall 50 metres later. We then climb alongside the wall for less than 50 metres to a small flat area, where the faint trail we've been following completely disappears. Twenty five metres further on, cairns indicate 'ways' to right and left. Ignoring the way to the right toward a *sitja* (it ends above heartrending cliffs), we bear left following three large cairns onto some very rough, very faint terraces (ESE). After crossing the first two 'terraces', we bear right to find a very faint trail through the woods to a wall (Wp.9 95M). Crossing the wall and bearing slightly left, we climb a tiny rise to come into sight of the wooded **Coll de s'Estret**. A faint path now descends (SSE) to another *sitja*-shelter-oven combination. Five metres behind the bread oven is the clear stony trail (Wp.10 100M) that leads up to **Col de s'Estret**. The pathfinding difficulties are over!

We turn left (away from the *coll*) and start climbing. The trail soon swings back towards the *coll* and climbs steadily in a southerly direction. Finally we clamber over a broken wall and, 50 metres later, come to the v-shaped bench at the *coll* (Wp.11 125M). Turning left, we follow the **Archduke's Path** onto the top of the cliffs, where it dips and rises along its most spectacular section.

After a long steady climb the path levels off in full view of **Puig Major** then bears right (ESE) towards the distinctive rocky knoll of **Puig Caragoli**. Just before the path dips down into the shallow depression before **Caragoli**, we find a large, metre high cairn on our left (Wp.12 155M) indicating the start of our descent. NOTE: if clouds have formed across the valley above **Deià** (which can happen alarmingly quickly) either return by the same route or take one of the easy descents to **Valldemossa** and catch a bus back. This is no place to be blundering about in the mist looking for a path.

To our left, a clear stony trail descends to another large cairn, where it seems to drop off the edge of the cliff – don't worry, it doesn't: this isn't a sick joke. Leaving the **Archduke's Path**, we follow the clear stony trail (NNE) down towards the first oaks, where the path again appears to drop off the edge of a cliff – this time it does, almost!

Bearing left after a long outcrop of rock next to a black/white private hunting sign (Wp.13 165M [there are no more waypoints due to poor GPS reception]), we follow the meticulously cairn-marked route down to a broad wooded traverse descending steeply below a first stretch of cliff. This and subsequent descents are all easy and rarely vertiginous, but take care as the rocks are unstable underfoot.

At first, the path has been built up in zigzags, but we soon descend directly along the face of the cliff (this sounds alarming, but the trees and 20 metre broad traverse mean it's a relatively easy descent) before bearing left to emerge from the first belt of trees onto a broad open stretch overlooking **Son Rullan** and **Sa Foradada**. Another built up stretch of path bears right, bringing us into a stand of mixed pine and oak, where we begin another long sloping traverse below cliffs and between trees. At the end of the second line of cliffs, the path narrows and doubles back to the left again, passing a large rock with a cairn on top and a man-made step with an old gatepost built into the rock.

We now come into the main oak forest, where we follow a long northward traverse, climbing slightly before continuing our descent. Ignoring a branch on the left, we turn sharp right, still following the cairns, to pass the final cliff face. We then zigzag steeply down through the woods to the bread-oven *sitja* at Wp.5 (205M) where we rejoin our outward route, forty minutes from the start. It's worth pausing on the way down in front of the rusty metal gates to look up and contemplate what is, from here, an evidently unfeasible descent.

A classic route winding along undulating coastline (take your swimming costume) and returning on one of the most popular paths in Mallorca. The path toward the end of the coastal walk is complicated, but well marked with red dots and cairns.

Short Version	Stroll	Extension
Cala de Deià to **Es Gall**, returning via the same route	**Camís de Sa Vinyetta** and **Ribassos** Loop	See Walks 1 & 8 for links to **Sóller** and **Port de Sóller**

Access: on foot from **Deià**

From the eastern end of **Deià**, just beyond the main car-park, we take the tarmac lane on the left, signposted 'GR Sóller/Cala de Deià Camí de Sa Vinyetta' (Wp.1 0M). At the end of the lane, we cross a stile onto a cobbled trail descending through olive terraces, crossing the road to the *cala* three times before joining it just above the **Camí des Ribassos** wooden bridge. Ignoring the GR-221 for **Sóller** on the right, we stay on the road down to the *cala*. At the chain blocking car access to the beach (Wp.2 30M), we can either bear right or descend to the beach, just above which long stone steps lead to an intersection where the path from Wp.2 runs onto a terrace. Bearing right behind a stone cabin on the eastern spur of the *cala*, we follow a low clifftop, then climb onto the next terrace when the path disappears.

At the first *mirador* (below a 'Cuidado con el perro' sign), we cross a watershed where a steel cable and ladder help us over a fallen tree (Wp.3 45M). Passing a picnic spot with a stone bench and round table, we climb to follow a high retaining wall, before crossing a wooden stile into a pine forest. A second stile brings us into woodland devastated by processionary caterpillars and *tomico*, a wood-boring bug that can kill a tree in 15 days flat! After a breach in a stone wall (Wp.4 70M), we descend to pass in front of a house next to the sea. The path then levels out, passing between another house and small *mirador*.

After the next stile (Wp.5 80M), we bear left to squeeze between the branches of a fallen tree and climb stone steps toward a steep earth cliff. The path across the cliff face has disappeared, obliging us to climb till we're level with the second of several deep terraces, where a newer path bears left. Another eroded stretch (passable at the time of writing, but not for long), means we have to zigzag up to cross the run-off channel causing the erosion, immediately after which we bear left to recover the main path. Passing between two cairns, we ignore a waymarked route climbing to the right and continue along the coastal path, crossing a dramatically riven gully. Once across the gully, we follow a fainter path marked with cairns every 10-15 metres.

After a winding climb round a logjam of dead trees, we again ignore waymarks to the right, and bear left below a huge boulder to climb onto a

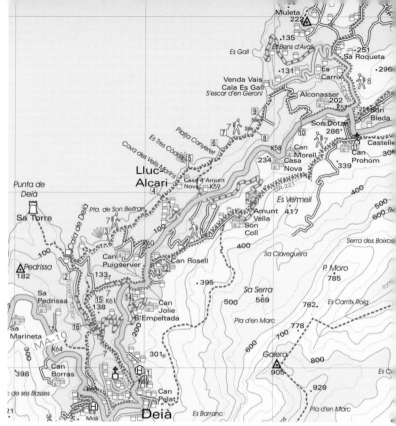

small wooded ridge. We then descend steeply alongside a wire fence, which we cross via a stile (Wp.6 95M) to rejoin the path cut by the logjam.

Cala de Deià

Crossing terraces of gnarled olive trees, we ignore old waymarks to the right yet again (Wp.7 100M) and follow newer waymarks and cairns down towards the sea. A sinuous path then climbs through a partially cleared tangle of dead trees to emerge at a stile (Wp.8 110M) behind orange and grey cliffs backed

by a deep fissure, where we descend half-left past a stone building.

The path becomes clearer and broader, traversing well-tended olive terraces to a padlocked gate and a stile (Wp.9 115M) leading onto a dirt track. We descend along the dirt track for 75 metres before bearing right on stone steps climbing into the woods, on the far side of which we join the concrete lane between the **Alconasser** estate and **Cala Es Gall** (called **Venda Vais** by locals).

Turning right, we climb steadily along the lane for twenty minutes before joining the MA-10 (Wp.10 145M).

Turning left and staying on the left-hand side to face the traffic, we follow the road for 500 metres, joining the GR221 as we pass the Bens d'Avall Restaurant turning (link to Walk 8), after which we cross the road to take the track in front of Cas Sord. After 15 metres, we bear left, climbing to Can Carabasseta and a tumbledown chapel, where we turn right on a cobbled path up to the Can Prohom farmhouse (Wp.11 165M).

After crossing the front yard of **Can Prohom**, we bear left on a dirt track for 150 metres before bearing left again on a wayposted path. The path goes through a green gate and crosses dense woodland before passing above two houses. After crossing an access track, we descend along a cobbled trail then climb newly paved steps to pass in front of **Son Coll** (**Posada del Rey Jaume**). Descending along dirt paths and ignoring a branch path to the left, we follow a broad low wall to emerge behind a new house (**Can Rosell**).

Bearing right on a roughly surfaced lane, we descend to join a smoother tarmac lane where indications for **Deià** and the GR have been scratched onto a concrete wall (Wp.12 210M). We can either follow the GR to the left on a cobbled path or bear right on the tarmac lane. Both emerge 50 metres later on the MA-10 (Wp.13 211M).

Unfortunately, our old route through the **Son Beltran** *urbanizacion* is no longer feasible, so we're obliged to turn left here and follow the GR along the road for 450 metres, walking on the left hand side of the road and staying very, very close to the rock. At a particularly heartrending left-hand bend, we skedaddle across the road as quick as we can to take a signposted cobbled trail (Wp.14 216M) that almost immediately joins a narrow lane. We follow the lane down past a large house, shortly after which the road becomes a dirt track, 25 metres along which we pass to the left of a farm building. 75 metres after passing a magnificent oak tree, the main track bears right and we fork left on a wayposted trail cutting across olive and carob terraces (Wp.15 221M). The trail then swings left and becomes a cobbled donkey trail dropping down into the **Cala de Deía** gorge to intersect with our outward route (Wp.16 227M). From here, we can either follow the GR back to **Deià** or, recommended, cross the bridge and continue on **Camí des Ribassos**.

To return to **Deià**, we take the wooden bridge (ten minutes from the *cala*) onto the **Camí des Ribassos**. The *camí* is cobbled at first, but soon dwindles to a dirt path climbing across terraces to join a paved way between houses and a lemon grove. The access track for the houses leads to a tarmac lane which we follow to the second Y-junction. Turning left past House No. 3, then left again in front of the **Deià Archaeological Museum**, we follow **Calle Felipe Bauza** up to the main road, 200 metres from our starting point, twenty-five minutes from the wooden bridge.

Walking on the popular **Muleta** plateau has got a good deal more congenial in recent years with a newly restored path, a newly negotiated right-of-way and new wayposts, the latter a godsend given that not all the landowners up here were conspicuously elated to see a walker stumbling into their property. Our new version of the itinerary makes use of all the new bits and some of the best of the old, climbing via the **Camí de Son Sales** and returning to **Port de Sóller** via the GR. The high refreshment rating comes of perfectly placed services en route and the presence of **Port de Sóller** bars and restaurants at the end.

Access: by car or on foot from **Port de Sóller**. To reach the start from **Port de Sóller**, walk along the seafront (W) and turn inland at the **Bar Las Delicias II** to pass the **Campo Sol** restaurant. **The Hotel Rocamar** is on the right 300 metres later.

Our itinerary starts 500 metres behind **Port de Sóller's Platja d'en Repic** at the derelict **Hotel Rocamar**, where there's a walking signpost for 'Deia, Soller, Muleta' (Wp.1 0M). The shell of the hotel makes for an unprepossessing start, but within 150 metres, the rough track cutting across its premises joins the GR above a Camina per Mallorca mapboard (Wp.2). Maintaining direction (SE), we ignore the sign for 'Muleta' and head for **Sóller**.

Forking right at the next junction (Wp.3 5M), we stay on the GR, which soon goes through a gate to follow a terrace path behind a private house. After climbing briefly below cliffs so heavily mottled they look like they've been camouflaged, we descend into the Son Sales valley, bearing right when our path feeds into a dirt track (Wp.4 17M), then right again a couple of hundred metres later when the track joins a narrow tarmac lane (Wp.5 20M), the **Camí de Son Sales**.

We follow the camí as it veers round to the right and goes through metal gates, staying on the main lane when a cobbled trail forks off to the right (Wp.6

26M). When the tarmac ends, we carry straight on for ten metres then fork right on a concrete track (Wp.7 31M). The concrete eventually gives way to dirt within sight of **Can Prohom**, the large, long farmhouse at the head of the valley. 150 metres later, we come to another, rougher stretch of concrete, at the end of which we leave the track, turning right on a narrow, wayposted path that goes through a gate and climbs across terraces in a southwesterly direction (Wp.8 41M). Immediately behind a small house, our path becomes an intermittently cobbled trail (Wp.9 47M). After crossing the edge of a cottage garden, our trail broadens as we climb through a stand of pine to join a broad dirt track, 100 metres from the **Son Bleda** hotel/bar/restaurant. On the far side of the hotel, we rejoin the GR on the MA10 (Wp.10 57M).

Turning right and taking great care (there's a nasty little bend ahead), we follow the MA10 for 125-metres then turn right on the **Bens d'Avall** lane (Wp.11). When the main lane climbs slightly then descends sharp left some 600 metres later, we turn right on a track (surfaced for the first 50 metres) (Wp.12 69M). Bearing right (Wp.13), then left (Wp.14 73M) at the next two junctions, we wind through olive

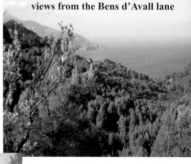
views from the Bens d'Avall lane

groves, individual trees looking so gnarled and ancient you can well believe some have been carbon dated BC.

Reaching another Camina per Mallorca mapboard, we ignore the turning on the left for the **Muleta** refuge and carry straight

millenary olive tree

on for **Port de Sóller** (Wp.15 81M). We also carry straight on at a crossroads 75 metres later (Wp.16) then fork right 25 metres after that (Wp.17) on a wayposted path that curves round the **Muleta de Cats Avinyons** farmhouse. Behind the farmhouse, we turn sharp left on a narrow path (Wp.18 86M) into another ancient olive grove.

views over Port de Soller after Wp.18

Following a broad trail peppered with cairns, we join a cobbled way that dips down into a swale then crosses a rise from where views open out over **Port de Sóller**r. Passing the **Muleta de ca s'Hereu** farmhouse (offering orange juice and pa amb oli) (Wp.19 94M), we trace a horseshoe curve round the next gully then descend to go through one more olive grove, beyond which a final steady descent brings us back to our starting point.

See the notes on GPS use and waypoints on pages 18-19.

1. Camí de Castello

Wp	N	E
1	39 45.9365	2 42.8905
2	39 45.6195	2 42.6895
3	39 45.5825	2 42.6845
4	39 45.5685	2 42.6565
5	39 45.5085	2 42.6135
6	39 45.2495	2 42.3195
7	39 45.5445	2 42.3045
8	39 45.7135	2 42.0375
9	39 45.7605	2 42.0075
10	39 45.7690	2 41.6959
11	39 46.0175	2 41.5215
12	39 46.3014	2 41.1119
13	39 46.2871	2 41.5943

2. Sa Comuna Ridge

Wp	N	E
1	39 42.6085	2 37.2395
2	39 42.5375	2 37.1955
3	39 42.4885	2 37.0685
4	39 42.4585	2 37.0255
5	39 42.2755	2 36.8185
6	39 42.2235	2 36.7635
7	39 42.2315	2 36.6615
8	39 42.0805	2 36.4355
9	39 42.0925	2 36.3945

3. The Archduke's Path from Valldemossa

(a) Mirador de ses Puntes

Wp	N	E
1	39 42.8682	2 37.3145
2	39 43.2654	2 37.2762
3	39 43.7040	2 37.3362
4	39 43.7490	2 37.1406
5	39 43.5360	2 36.7278

(b) via Fontanelles

Wp	N	E
1	39 42.9702	2 37.3788
2	39 43.2852	2 38.0232
3	39 43.5642	2 38.0910
4	39 43.6992	2 38.3196
5	39 43.9146	2 38.8392
6	39 43.7970	2 38.1108
7	39 43.5792	2 37.4784
8	39 43.7040	2 37.3362

4. Teix from Valldemossa

Wp	N	E
1	39 42.8275	2 37.7805
2	39 42.9775	2 37.3785
3	39 43.0535	2 38.5505
4	39 42.8235	2 38.3525
5	39 42.8325	2 38.4005
6	39 42.8735	2 38.5985
7	39 42.8625	2 38.6175
8	39 42.8695	2 38.6305
9	39 42.9155	2 38.6735
10	39 43.0045	2 38.8455
11	39 43.0765	2 38.8375
12	39 43.1125	2 38.8765
13	39 43.1335	2 38.9505
14	39 43.2015	2 38.9985
15	39 43.2005	2 39.0155
16	39 43.3745	2 39.1475
17	39 43.5348	2 39.4020
18	39 43.6110	2 39.3804
19	39 43.8792	2 39.6816
20	39 43.8810	2 39.1368
21	39 43.5485	2 39.1695

5. Sa Foradada

(a) The Lost Path

Wp	N	E
1	39 43.2106	2 35.6020
2	39 43.7832	2 36.0546
3	39 44.1432	2 36.4296
4	39 44.4612	2 36.7638
5	39 44.5482	2 36.8760
6	39 44.9682	2 37.4220
7	39 45.1134	2 37.4958
8	39 45.3528	2 37.3404

(b) from Son Marroig

Wp	N	E
1	39 45.0768	2 37.7574
2	39 45.1194	2 37.4928
3	39 45.3540	2 37.3422

6. The Archduke's Path from Deià

Wp	N	E
1	39 44.7900	2 38.6304
2	39 44.6958	2 38.4282
3	39 44.5326	2 38.2584
4	39 44.4204	2 38.1438
5	39 44.3136	2 38.0610
6	39 44.3166	2 37.9014
7	39 44.1588	2 37.7268
8	39 44.0850	2 37.6884
9	39 44.0250	2 37.5702
10	39 43.9518	2 37.5618
11	39 43.7202	2 37.3488
12	39 43.8696	2 37.9332
13	39 44.0370	2 37.0334

7. Deià - Can Prohom - Deià

Wp	N	E
1	39 44.9388	2 38.9058
2	39 45.5502	2 38.4960
3	39 45.7050	2 38.7294
4	39 45.9594	2 39.1398
5	39 46.1322	2 39.3438
6	39 46.2300	2 39.5946
7	39 46.2924	2 39.6750
8	39 46.3428	2 39.8468
9	39 46.4016	2 39.8982
10	39 46.3944	2 40.1814
11	39 46.2900	2 40.5966
12	39 45.5874	2 39.0684
13	39 45.5795	2 39.0305
14	39 45.4765	2 38.8505
15	39 45.4285	2 38.6025
16	39 45.2355	2 38.5785

8. La Muleta

Wp	N	E
1	39 47.1685	2 41.6835
2	39 47.1095	2 41.7535
3	39 47.0415	2 41.8505
4	39 46.7835	2 41.7415
5	39 46.7005	2 41.6265
6	39 46.6785	2 41.4155
7	39 46.6795	2 41.2365
8	39 46.5815	2 40.9115
9	39 46.4895	2 40.7935
10	39 46.4135	2 40.5985
11	39 46.4785	2 40.5725
12	39 46.7955	2 40.4525
13	39 46.8765	2 40.4985
14	39 46.9005	2 40.6225
15	39 47.1125	2 40.7775
16	39 47.1005	2 40.8325
17	39 47.0945	2 40.8565
18	39 47.0325	2 40.8785
19	39 47.0895	2 41.1715

FROM THE GOLDEN SHELL TO THE SEA OF ROCK

Though friendly and helpful, I suspect the people of **Sóller** mistrust outsiders. I suggest this only because the town's one-way system is like something out of an M.C. Escher drawing. Things look straightforward enough when you arrive, but venture into town by car and you'll find yourself going in completely the wrong direction to get where you want to go. Either the locals are out to protect their privacy or they've decided the town's narrow streets can only cope with local traffic and have elaborated a road system so complex it baffles all but the most stubborn tourist - all to the good, as this is a place to explore on foot. Apart from the museum, Botanical Gardens and a few distinguished buildings, there's not much in the way of classic sightseeing, but it's a delightful little town of sunny, bustling streets and shady peaceful alleyways, with several good bars and restaurants, and a central plaza, ideal for whiling away an afternoon watching the world go by - and when you tire of the human parade, a short stroll to the edge of town unfolds the fabulous spectacle of the surrounding mountains.

If you approach **Sóller** from the south, you'll be confronted by a toll tunnel, a boon for local people, reducing what was, with repetition, a tiresome, time-consuming climb to a straightforward, fast road. However, if you're not in a hurry, take the old road snaking over the **Coll de Sóller**. The bends are interminable, but so, from certain strategic points, are the attractive views, even on a cloudy day. And if you don't have a car, the nonagenarian train from **Palma** is an essential excursion.

Virtually anywhere else in Spain, the plain between **Sóller** and the port would be a dense forest of tower blocks or a broad sweep of villas. There's some development, but the passion for oranges, orchards and gardens has saved this area, and there are several attractive strolls to be done. **Port de Sóller** is very much a tourist resort with the usual array of bars and restaurants and car-hire outlets, but on an eminently manageable scale, at once peaceable and affordable, used as much by locals as visitors.

The MA-10 heading east from **Sóller** is one of the island's great drives/cycle rides. Snaking its way up past the celebrated **Mirador de ses Barques**, it climbs towards the daunting summit of **Puig Major**, an increasingly dramatic gulf opening out between the road and the long ridge sealing the **Cúber** and **Ofre** valleys. After the **Sa Bassa** *área recreativa* a sea of rock unfurls around us, announcing the approach of the first of two tunnels boring through the fringes of **Puig Major**. Beyond the tunnel, we are in the heart of the sea, with the white crest of **Puig Major** towering over a long trough backed by bubbling waves of rock. With their usual pragmatism, the Mallorcans have taken advantage of the terrain to turn this spot into the region's principal water storage point and once again, practical considerations have had an aesthetically pleasing outcome. Girdled by small mountains, **Cúber** reservoir is a picture postcard lake, a metallic mirror changing colour from steely green to deep aquamarine according to the humours of the sky. After **Cúber** we begin the long eastern descent, passing **Gorg Blau** reservoir (lower down but the source of most of the water in the **Cúber**) and going through the second tunnel, where the wave breaks, and a cascade of rock tumbles down toward

Pollença. First though, there's an essential detour to the left, the extraordinary descent to **Sa Calobra** and **Cala Tuent**, which in a couple of kilometres, passes through a narrow defile just above **Nus de Corbata** - The Tie Knot. One glance at the map tells you all you need to know about the subsequent descent. No matter how many mountain tracks or corniche routes you've done, you won't fail to be impressed by this road, frequently so tightly coiled it resembles a partially unravelled spring. And if you can take your eye off the road for a fleeting second, you'll see an equally impressive spectacle on either side, a gallery of remarkably varied rock, some delicately fluted, some mimicking the phantasmagoric shapes of Dali's Cap Creus, one striking declivity pinching the road like a peg, all of it quite stunning, especially in the twilight. The road is not for nervous drivers, though, boasting more bends than a plateful of spaghetti. Professional drivers seem perfectly relaxed as they swing their buses (not to mention a ceiling full of screaming sightseers) round disturbingly tight corners, but given that you're the one who must

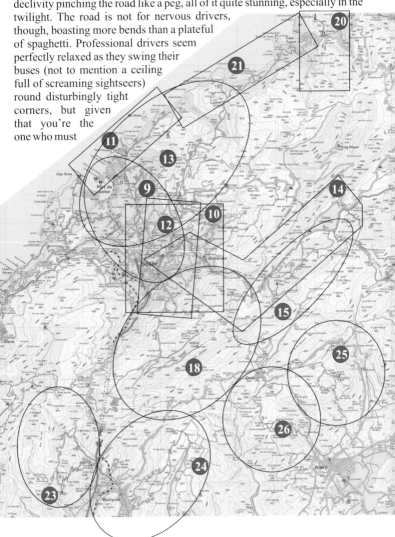

give way, often in places where there doesn't appear to be any 'way' into which to 'give', visiting motorists may wish to go early or late - above all, avoid this road at midday when countless coaches carry their cargo down to the feeding places at **Sa Calobra**.

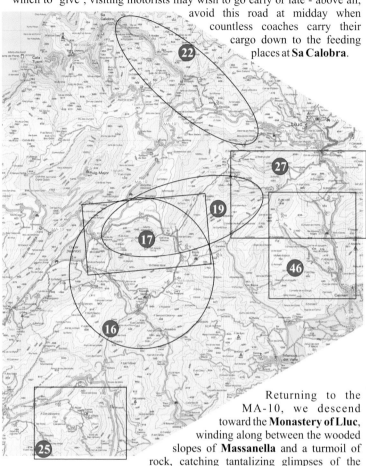

Returning to the MA-10, we descend toward the **Monastery of Lluc**, winding along between the wooded slopes of **Massanella** and a turmoil of rock, catching tantalizing glimpses of the immense trenches of the **Gorg Blau** and **Lluc** torrents, backed by the massif of **Puig Roig**, identifiable by the isolated **Quartel de Carabiners** barracks. The two torrents merge below the **Escorca** restaurant to form the single, undisputable natural wonder of the island, the **Torrente de Pareis**, a deep, narrow gorge debouching at **Sa Calobra** (inspiring the convoy of coaches mentioned earlier) and luring canyoning aficionados from all over Europe.

Parallel to all this drama, on the southern side of the **Tramuntana** between **Bunyola** and **Caimari** is an altogether gentler but no less beguiling landscape of pleasant, fertile valleys fringed with attractive woods and punctuated by impressive limestone escarpments. Long neglected by conventional tourists, its popularity is increasing making it quite crowded at weekends, but there are some great walks here and the tiny, winding lanes linking the villages are a gift to cyclists and motorists who are in no hurry to arrive.

A gentle stroll on quiet country lanes, dirt tracks, and ancient cobbled ways, ideal for a day off when you still fancy a breath of fresh air. Despite the proximity of the beach resort and holiday homes, this is still very much working countryside, as you will see if you happen to be here in autumn when stacks of sacks of carob pods line the terraces awaiting collection. The route is clearly sign and wayposted throughout.

*very gentle inclines

Access: on foot from **Sóller**. To reach the start from **Sóller's** central **Plaza de sa Constitució**, take **Carrer de sa Lluna** next to the BBVA bank, then second left on **Carrer de la Victoria 11 Maig**. Go straight on at the crossroads and bear right at the bridge (signposted 'Piscina Municipal') into **Avenguda d'Asturies**. The football ground is on the right 150 metres later.

From **Sóller** football ground (Wp.1 0M), we follow the 'Port Sóller' road for 100 metres, forking left just after the **Club Petanca** (Wp.2) and taking the middle tine of the triple fork 300 metres later (Wp.3 8M), heading toward a church with a distinctive square tower. Carrying straight on at the church (Wp.4 11M), we leave the town behind as we stroll along an increasingly narrow and attractive lane leading to the MA10. Crossing the road carefully (cars whip round the bend at a hell of a lick), we follow the **Finca Can Penya** lane (Wp.5 18M) for 150 metres, then fork left into the **Camí de sa Pages** (Wp.6).

After passing in front of a row of terraced houses, we climb along a cobbled trail that feeds into a track which we follow for 175 metres (NW). When the track bears right behind a house, we fork left on a wayposted path (Wp.7). The path crosses then rejoins a dirt track (Wp.8 40M) on which we maintain direction (N) for a gentle climb to the **Coll d'en Borrassar**, where we carry straight on at a Y-junction (the left hand branch) (Wp.9 44M) and remain on the track at the junction with a signposted path descending to the left 50 metres later (Wp.10).

the terraced houses

stacked sacks of Carob pods

We now simply stay on the main track, passing **Can Alfonso** (orange juice available) and enjoying unfolding views of the **Balitx** massif, until we reach the MA2124 (Wp.11 63M). Turning left, we follow the road for a kilometre and a half down to the roundabout at the northern entrance to the new **Port de Sóller** tunnel (Wp.12 80M).

tunnel of a different order

Turning left, we follow a signposted trail shadowing the tunnel access road. Just before the tunnel entrance, we pass a tunnel of a different order, and our path veers left to climb through the woods. Ignoring a cairn-marked shortcut, we stick with the wayposted path, zigzagging up across retaining

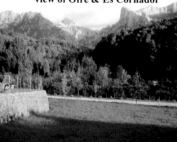
view of Ofre & Es Cornador

walls amid delightful woodland to reach a boundary wall (Wp.13 90M). The path runs alongside the wall then goes through a couple of gates before rejoining our outward route at Wp.10 (99M). We return the same way with the option of staying on the dirt track at

Wp.8 and following the **Can Penya** lane back to Wp.6.

NB For an interesting alternative ending (discovered by chance after we had finished our main research) follow the **Can Penya** lane then turn left 200 metres before Wp.6 on the **Camí de ses Alzines** dirt track (signposted with a blue plaque on the wall) (Wp.Alt1). The cami, which becomes a path during the middle section, emerges 500 metres later on the MA10 beside the **Sa Teulera Restaurant** (Wp.Alt2), from where we simply cross the road and follow the **Camí de ses Argiles** and the **Camí de Can Domatiga** to rejoin our outward route at Wp.3.

10 THREE VILLAGES + ONE THUNDERING GREAT CLIMB

Essentially, this itinerary is two loops tacked onto one another and can easily be broken into several smaller walks. The basic loop is the classic tour from **Sóller** of **Binibassi**, **Fornalutx** and **Biniaraix**, a lovely, bucolic stroll that should be within everyone's range. On top of that, the energetic have the option of climbing a superb donkey trail to **Sa Bassa** and the **Mirador de ses Barques**, from where another donkey trail brings us back to **Fornalutx**. The climb to **Sa Bassa** is via the **Camí de s'Alzina Fumadora**, named after a large, shady Holm Oak under which everyone used to stop for a fag break.

4* **4H** ** 14 km 500m / 500m 5

*Short Versions (a) 4, (b) 2   **Short Versions (a) 3hours, (b) 1½ hours

---

Short Version:- There's an interesting short walk to be done linking the present itinerary with Walk 12. Follow Walk 12 to Wp.4. Turn right, then fork left 30-metres later to join a lovely path that follows a contour for a little over 30M before emerging on the MA-10 at the junction with the Fornalutx road. 50 metres down the Fornalutx road we join the present itinerary just above Wp.8.

Access: on foot from **Sóller**

From **Sóller's** central **Plaza de sa Constitució**, we take **Carrer de sa Lluna** next to the BBVA bank, then turn second left on **Carrer de la Victoria 11 Maig**.
Carrying straight on at the crossroads, we bear right at the bridge (signposted

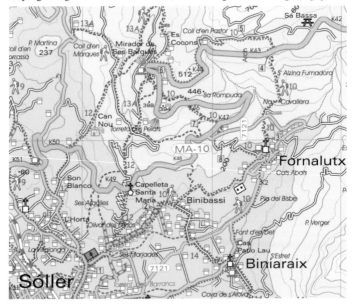

'Piscina Municipal') into **Avenguda d'Asturies**, then turn right at the football field on the **Biniaraix/Fornalutx** road (Wp.1 10M).

When the road crosses **Pont de Can Rave**, we turn left on a tarmac lane (following the GR), which promptly swings right, passing two signposted branches (see Walk 12). Bearing left at the end of the lane (Wp.2 25M), we climb a partially cobbled trail to the idyllic hamlet of **Binibassi**. Ignoring the access road, we bear left (signposted 'Fornalutx') beside a trough-like culvert to take the footpath out of the hamlet.

After going through a green gate, we follow a broad trail across terraces before bearing right at a waypost to take a narrow path marked with red dots. We immediately go through another gate and bear right down a stepped descent onto a path running alongside a high retaining wall. The path leads onto a tarmac and concrete lane passing terraces. The lane dips then climbs past the **Fornalutx** cemetery before leading into the village itself (45M). Ignoring the road descending to the right, we continue straight ahead, passing the kindergarten to join **Carrer de Sol**, from where **Carrer de sa Plaza** leads into the main village square (50M). If you don't intend doing the full walk, return to **Carrer de Sol** after exploring the village.

For the full walk

Camí de s'Alzina Fumadora

We climb the steps next to **Fornalutx** church and, from **Carrer des Vent**, take **Carrer de Tramuntana** up to the **Camí de s'Alzina Fumadora / Sa Comuna** (Wp.3 55M). Climbing past hillside smallholdings, we cross the **Fornalutx** access road, where we pass above a small fenced reservoir and take a concrete track, 30 metres along which, a signpost indicates our donkey trail on the left.

For the next half-hour, we simply follow the cobbled trail, if something that climbs so relentlessly can be described as 'simple'. The long, shallow steps look easy, but they're deceptively steep and there's every chance you'll reach the top wishing never to see another step again.

However, the effort is amply rewarded with superb views across the intricate jigsaw of terraces climbing towards the **Ofre** ridge to the south. After crossing an access track, we climb steadily to go through a wire gate. The climb gets even steeper, passing a waypost and zigzagging up across terraces, before finally emerging on the MA-10, just east of km 43 at a signpost for 'Fornalutx 45M' (Wp.4 90M).

Fifty metres to the right, we take a signposted path ('Pla de sa Bassa') crossing a stile then a *sitja*, where the path broadens to a trail climbing to join a rough dirt track behind a green fire-fighting reservoir (Wp.5 105M).

Turning left, we follow the track round the base of **Sa Bassa**, going through the natural gateway of **Coll d'en Pastor**, before descending through rubble strewn switchbacks to one of the **Es Cocons** access gates. We bear left, down to a second gate, possibly locked but an easy climb over the left hand pillar, onto the MA-10 at km 43.7.

Unfortunately, we now have over a kilometre on the road to descend to the **Mirador de ses Barques**. At the *mirador* car park, we cross onto the right hand side of the road and, as the road bears left, go through the gap between the stone and metal crash barriers (Wp.6 140M), just behind which a signpost indicates the common start of the **Sóller/Fornalutx/Port de Sóller** paths.

After descending along a narrow path with a steel cable handrail, we go through a bedstead gate and turn left to rejoin the MA-10 100 metres later. 150 metres along the road, we bear left on a dirt track signposted 'Fornalutx/Costa d'en Nico'. The track passes two houses before being blocked by a gate, where we turn right to join the cobbled donkey trail down to **Fornalutx**. The first narrow stretch descends directly to the road. 50 metres to the left, we take a signposted concrete track for 10 metres until a waypost indicates the next stage of the donkey trail descending to our left. Taking care not to drift off onto the terraces, we follow the donkey trail until it runs into a broader stony track (Wp.7 170M). We bear left for 30 metres before branching right on cobbled steps to cut out a bend. 50 metres further along the track, another section of donkey trail cuts out a second bend, after which the track descends to cross the MA-10 (173M) for the last time.

On the other side of the road, we follow a concrete driveway behind a house then cross the gravelled area in front of a carport. We then cross the **Fornalutx** access road onto a tarmac lane, which we follow till a waypost (Wp.8 180M) indicates a shortcut avoiding a bend. We now repeat this procedure, following and crossing the lane five times. Behind the first house on the outskirts of **Fornalutx**, we leave the lane and take the steps behind the house down to **Carrer de la Pau**. Bearing left we come back to **Carrer de Sol**.

To return to Sóller from Fornalutx
We turn right on **Carrer de Sol** and descend to the main road in front of the principal **Fornalutx** car-park. Bearing right, we follow the road past the **Per Amunt Restaurant**, then bear left on **Carrer Mallorca** (signposted 'Sóller a Peu'), cutting a bend in the road. After a second shortcut lane, we follow the road for 500 metres, taking the second turning on the left, a narrow lane that brings us into **Biniaraix** (210M). Turning right on the **Carrer de Sant Josep**, we walk through the small square in front of the Bar/Bodega and follow the 'Sóller a Peu' signs before steps lead down to the road, which we follow back to **Sóller** (225M). Ignoring traffic signs suggesting the town centre is on our right (it ain't), we carry straight on to rejoin **Carrer de sa Lluna**.

N.B. Alternatively, we can follow the new route of the GR to rejoin our outward route at **Binibassi**. See Walk 14 for details.

11 THE ULTIMATE PICNIC WALK: TORRE PICADA & SA ILLETA

This is the ultimate picnic walk, climbing to the **Torre Picada** watchtower above **Port de Sóller** for coffee and biscuits, then following a lovely corniche path to a *sitja* below the **Puig Balitx** cliffs for an aperitif, before finally descending to a superb look-out point over **Sa Illeta** island for the main picnic - come prepared! A good family walk.

2 — 3¼ H ** — 14 km — 250m / 250m — ⇔ — 0

** + 20 minutes for the **Punta Larga** extension

Access: on foot from **Port de Sóller**.

From **Port de Sóller** sea front, we take the road toward the new tunnel next to **Hotel Generoso** (Wp.1 0M) into into **Avenguida 11 de Maig** and **Carrer de Belgica**. After a steady climb, the road swings sharp left (Wp.2 10M) and we maintain direction on a narrow tarmac lane. The lane climbs steadily then steeply between olive terraces before swinging sharp right at the **Coll d'es Figueral** in front of a gate and stone wall with steps over it (Wp.3 20M). For our coffee break at the *torre*, we cross the wall and immediately turn left onto the cairn-marked path between the trees.

The path climbs gently, passing several shortcuts, before emerging on a dirt track just below a T-junction backed by mounds of rubble. Taking the right hand branch of the T, we climb the broad track till it dwindles to a trail leading to the **Torre Picada** (Wp.4 30M) from where we have fine views along the coast and inland. On the nearside of the tower, a trodden path leads down to a grassy platform that's ideal for our coffee break. To return to the *coll*, we retrace our steps and, 75 metres after the stone gateway to the tower, where the trail widens to a track under the pines, bear left on a narrow, waymarked path. Rejoining the main track lower down, we bear left again and follow the track back to the *coll* (40M).

We now continue along the tarmac lane, which soon levels out, bringing us into fine views of the **Penyal Bernat** pinnacle and **Sa Illeta**, and passing a sign for 'Es Coll des Ille, Privat', shortly after which the tarmac ends and we continue on a dirt track.

... to pass below a cabin ...

After a tight chicane, a cairn indicates a shortcut climbing across the terraces to our right (Wp.5 55M) and re-crossing the dirt track higher up. At the second junction with the dirt track, we bear left to pass below a cabin. We now continue along the dirt track, passing the idyllically situated and well-restored main house and several satellite cabins.

Shortly after passing the drive to **Can Bardi**, we come to a locked green gate where cairns to the right indicate a way through the fence above the gate (Wp.6 70M).

We then walk along a retaining wall for 20 metres and, ignoring the main trail that continues through a wall-gate with a stone hinge bracket, bear left to descend through another gap in the wall, just after which there's a Y-junction of paths. The branch on the left is the way down to our picnic spot, but for the moment we continue on the main path, descending gently through the woods. The path comes into fine views of the cliffs below **Es Joncar** and passes a slightly vertiginous stretch before ending in a *sitja* (Wp.7 90M), just in time for an aperitif. (N.B. The waymarked routes continuing from this *sitja* both involve some precarious scrambling and are <u>not</u> recommended.)

Refreshed by our aperitif, we retrace our steps to the branch path just after Wp.6 and take the lower path descending steadily on a slippery carpet of pine needles to a stand of half-a-dozen water barrels fed by a spring (Wp.8 125M). After eating our fill and gazing on the great crocodile's snout of **Sa Illeta**, where hundreds of seagulls swirl overhead like swarms of midges, we return by the same route.

If you want to bathe on the way back, take the narrow path descending north from **Coll d'es Figueral**. (It's possible to make a loop using the broad track heading NE, but this doesn't add much and is only recommended for those wishing to while away an afternoon exploring the headland). When the path comes into a slight rise, soon blocked by fallen pine, bear left and follow the gully down to a lovely little inlet, ideal for rock-bathing in calm seas.

This pleasant short walk follows two classic cobbled trails climbing towards the **Mirador de ses Barques**. Despite recent wayposting, these routes are little used nowadays, which is a pity as they provide a perfect introduction to the peaceful countryside around **Sóller**.

Extension	Stroll
To the **Mirador de ses Barques** and **Port de Sóller** (see Walk 13a)	To Wp.3 then descend via the **Costa d'en Flassada** path, which arrives in **Sóller** a little way north of the football ground.

Access: on foot from **Sóller**   **Short Version** - see Walk 10.

We start as per Walk 10, following the **Fornalutx** road past the football field and turning left at the **Pont de Can Rave**. Ignoring the concrete track 150 metres later (**Camí de ses Marjades**), we turn left 50 metres further along onto the **Camí de sa Capelleta** (Wp.1 15M). The path climbs behind two houses and crosses a dirt track. At a second junction with the track, we bear right and, 100 metres later, turn left to recover the path.

Capelleta de Santa María

We then cross the track three more times before joining the final stepped ascent (briefly interrupted by the track) to the **Capelleta de Santa Maria** (Wp.2 27M).The chapel is a nicely proportioned building and benches outside provide a pleasant spot for a breather, though the interior is chiefly remarkable for its egg-box wall (NOT a metaphor!).

Continuing our ascent from the chapel gates, we cross the MA-10 onto a clear well-marked path that climbs steadily, occasionally alongside, occasionally crossing a concrete track before joining the **Costa d'en Flassada** path (Wp.3 35M).

Bearing right, we continue climbing between terraces, coming into fine views of the **Mitx Dia** on our right.

At the next junction with the concrete track, we bear right to recover the wayposted path 30 metres later. Steady climbing brings us to another signposted concrete track (Wp.4 45M) where we join the descent of Walk 13a. Bearing left (in the direction of **Port de Sóller**), we contour round the mountain, following the track as the concrete gives way to dirt. After 500 metres, the track swings right, climbing through another concreted section (Wp.5 55M).

For the **Mirador de ses Barques**, bear right and follow the waymarked walking trail visible just above us (Walk 13a Wp.2). For **Port de Sóller**, bear right and stay on the track. Otherwise, turn left to descend the initially grassy then cobbled path between terraces.

After going through a gate and passing a small spring, the path runs into a track descending to a large farmhouse (**Can Nou**), just below which we bear left, off the tarmac driveway, onto a grassy path marked by blue arrows (Wp.6 65M). Going through a light wire-mesh gate, we recover the cobbled trail and cross more terraces. After a sturdier metal gate, we continue our steady descent down to the MA-10.

Crossing the road, we take the concrete driveway down to **Can Bisbal**, where a final cobbled stretch leads into a concrete and tarmac lane (**Camí Vell de Balitx**), which ends at a T-junction with the **Camí de Son Blanco**. We turn right at the T-junction, then left at the next T-junction and follow the **Camí de ses Argiles** back past the football ground and into **Sóller**.

13 THE MIRADOR DE SES BARQUES AND THE BALITX VALLEY

Two walks for the price of one here, our previous approach to the **Balitx** valley being reduced to an alternative short walk from **Coll d'en Marques**, while the main itinerary explores the valley in full, climbing to the **Torre de na Seca** martello tower, from where we enjoy some of the finest views on the island. The two itineraries can be combined and further extended by following Walk 21 in reverse for the classic linear route to **Cala Tuent**, returning to **Port de Sóller** by boat.

a. The Mirador de ses Barques from Coll d'en Marques

Access: by car or on foot (add 80M return) from **Port de Sóller** via the MA2124. There's parking for two small cars on the northern side of the coll.

From **Coll d'en Marques** (Wp.1 0M), just as the road starts to descend toward **Sóller**, we take the tarmac lane on the left, bearing right 30 metres from the road on an unmarked cobbled trail. After going through a first gate, we climb steeply to a second gate, beyond which we continue climbing until the trail bears right and we join a dirt track.

Bearing left, we climb towards a new house, just before which we turn right onto a cairn-marked path. 50 metres along this path, we go through a gate under the natural arch of a carob tree, beyond which we walk between crumbling retaining walls, initially on the level, then climbing slightly to a point where a steel cable has been set in the rocks as a handrail. 30 metres later, we join a dirt track beside a small concrete cabin. Maintaining direction (SE), we follow the track behind the cabin, going through two green gates, the second next to an old farmhouse.

Cami Vell de Balitx

The track then descends through a concreted bend before winding along the contour line to a second concreted bend (Wp.2 25M), where we turn left on a broad cobbled path. At the second of two large metal gates, we ignore a branch to the right and maintain direction (N) to join a dirt track (Wp.3 35M). Bearing left for a few metres, we recover the path, which climbs via a cobbled stretch to intersect with Walk 13b at Wp.3 (Wp.4 45M). Crossing the **Balitx** track, we take the signposted path (the **Camí Vell de Balitx**) for the 'Mirador de ses Barques'. After crossing a small rise, we bear right on a wayposted trail descending to the *mirador* (Wp.5 55M).

On the far side of the mirador carpark, we take the 'Fornalutx, Port Sóller' path, which descends to a signposted junction of routes for 'Fornalutx' and 'Sóller'. Opting for the **Sóller** path, we descend steadily through a lovely natural tunnel formed by a deeply embedded cobbled path and a high canopy of oak trees. Joining a stony track, we bear left (Wp.6 65M), passing a gate topped with metal letters spelling out 'Es Figueral', 100 metres after which, we leave the track (Wp.7 70M), taking a waymarked path below the house on the left.

When the path emerges on a dirt track, we turn left then immediately right to join a concrete track, 10 metres along which a signpost indicates 'Port Sóller' to the right. After passing the entrance to **Ses Moncades**, the concrete deteriorates and eventually gives way to dirt. The track winds along the contour before climbing slightly to a sharp right hand bend where it is concreted again. Ignoring the waymarked path on the left, we stay on the track as it climbs to rejoin our outward route at Wp.2 (85M).

b. Torre de na Seca from the Mirador de ses Barques

Access: via car or bus

Our itinerary begins at the **Mirador de ses Barques** carpark on the MA10 east of **Sóller** on a stepped path signposted 'Cala Tuent, Sa Costera, Balitx' (Wp.1 0M). Until Wp.10 the walk is clearly wayposted, so the book can be stowed after a preliminary perusal. Given that the linear route to **Cala Tuent** is very, very popular with organized hiking groups, it's best to set out early or late to avoid the crowds.

the cobbled trail

After a brief climb along a charming cobbled trail (the **Camí Vell de Balitx**), we emerge on a concrete track in front of a small house (Wp.2 5M), where we bear left. Going through a gateway, we descend across olive terraces to join the main **Balitx** dirt track, where we bear right (Wp.3 18M) and stroll alongside the immaculately tended fields of the **Balitx de Dalt** (Upper Balitx) estate, beyond which we can see the **Torre de na Seca** on the far side of the valley.

200 metres after going through a gateway in front of the **Balitx de Dalt** farmhouse,

the main track doubles back to the left and a branch forks off to the right, between which we carry straight on along the cobbled *camí vell* (Wp.4 43M). The trail passes two springs before rejoining the main track beside the ruin of **Balitx d'en Mig** (in the middle) (Wp.5 50M). Continuing on the track, we descend into the spectacular trough of the **Balitx** valley.

100 metres above a small house, we leave the track, descending slightly to the left to recover the *camí vell*, signposted 'Balitx d'Avall, Tuent' (Wp.6 63M).

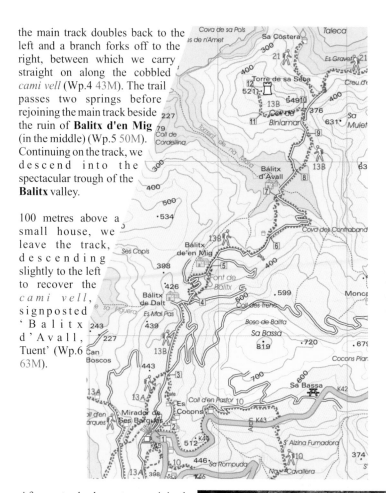

After a steady descent, we rejoin the main track (Wp.7 76M) just above the **Balitx d'Avall** (lower) farmhouse famous for its orange juice, which, given the location, is very reasonably priced at 2 euros a glass. If the courtyard's not packed with a guided hiking party, it's well worth stopping for a glass and to inspect the collection of farm implements in the bar area. The people are friendly, too, despite living on a route that can, at its busiest, resemble a motorway.

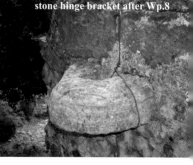

stone hinge bracket after Wp.8

Crossing the torrent below the farm, we leave the track again, turning right at a signposted junction (Wp.8 82M) to recover the cobbled *camí vell* as it zigzags up the wooded terraces of the valley's northeastern flank. After a steady slog, we rejoin the now very rough track (Wp.9 97M) for the final climb toward the **Coll de Biniamar**.

At the last bend immediately below the coll, we leave the crowds behind and turn left (Wp.10 103M) on a broad trail behind a waypost indicating that the standard route continues over the coll.

Heading west, we follow a contour, passing some wonderful rock formations while superb views of the **Balitx** valley open out behind us. After going through a gate, we climb to a turning circle at the end of the trail, where cairns and green waymarks indicate the steep climb onto the ridge (Wp.11 112M).

view from the torre

This stretch is off-path, but though there's abundant *carritx* and the *torre* isn't visible until the last moment, pathfinding is not a problem. The way becomes clearer, and possibly a little steeper toward the top, but don't despair because the views from the *torre* (Wp.12 127M) would justify double the effort.

We return via the same route with the option of following the track at Wps.9, 7, 5, & 3 for a moderately easier gradient, and maybe even a lift if you're lucky!

N.B. There's a mildly deranged document available on the internet approved by the Consell de Mallorca (who really ought to know better) suggesting there is a cairn-marked way down the northern side of the ridge from the *torre* to **Sa Costera**. There isn't. I've got the lacerated knees and disgruntled wife to prove it. Rarely have I endured such an unpleasant descent, the occasion I came down the Atlas mountains with a Great Dane draped round my shoulders not excluded. One or two cairns remain, but the way has disappeared. GPS users will note a jump in the track file between Wps.12 & 10 where I edited out our suffering.

L'Ofre is the distinctive conical peak southeast of **Sóller** that, from a distance, appears to be mantled in a dense cloak of trees except for a small tonsure on top. Though not particularly high, it's such a distinctive summit that its ascent has become something of a classic and it can get a little crowded at times, but one shouldn't be too sniffy about things that are popular, since they're often popular for a reason. In this instance, that tonsure really is a spectacular little eyrie, offering fabulous views of the more dramatic summits to the west ringing the **Ofre** farm. Get there early, though, otherwise it's elbow room only.

Another classic is the descent to **Sóller** on the GR221 as it follows Mallorca's most famous cobbled donkey trail, which we offer as an extension of the basic itinerary for those arriving by bus. The 900 metre descent from **Coll de l'Ofre** to **Sóller** takes about two hours.

NB The new GR route from **Biniaraix** to **Sóller** was recorded separately resulting in a difference of .080 seconds between Wp.E3 and the new *lavadero* waypoint. The new route back to **Sóller** is clearly sign and wayposted, but if you wish to use GPS, note that the **Biniaraix** to **Sóller** stretch is in separate WP/track files with a BS prefix for 'Biniaraix to Soller'.

Stroll: a simple tour round the reservoir is very pleasant when the weather is too hot or too wild to contemplate anything more arduous.

Extension: **Es Barranc** descent to **Sóller** (see text)

Access: by car and bus. Our itinerary starts at the **Cúber** parking area/bus stop at km34 of the MA10.

Ofre seen from the reservoir

From the **Cúber** parking area (Wp.1 0M), we contour round the reservoir, either via the GR on its northern side, or the tarmac lane/dirt track on the southern shore. At the far end of the lake, we go through the gates into the **Ofre** estate (Wp.2 28M) from where we can see the conelike summit of the same name.

1200 metres later, in front of the uninhabited **Binimorat** farmhouse, the GR forks right, leaving the main dirt track (Wp.3 34M) to follow a broad, intermittently cobbled trail that climbs gently to the **Coll de l'Ofre** (Wp.4 45M), where there's a tall metal crucifix planted in a pile of stones and fine views open out toward the summits surrounding the **Ofre** farmhouse.

Turning left, initially off-path, we head for a black and white hunting rectangle and a red *'Camino Particular Prohibido el Paso'* sign (don't worry, this really is a classic, everybody ignores the sign!), behind which a rough track winds through a bend before climbing in an easterly direction. The track eventually levels out within sight of **Coll d'es Cards** (up to our right) before emerging in an open flat grassy area directly below the coll.

Coll de l'Ofre

On the far side of the flat grassy area, we intersect with Walk 15 at an inverted Y-junction (Wp.5 55M). Turning right, we climb to the **Coll d'es Cards** (Wp.6 58M). Bearing right, we cross the rocks to the left of a metal pylon, behind which cairns mark a rough trail pieced together from patches of sheep paths. Keeping an eye out for the cairns, we climb steadily (SW) to a junction with the southern approach (Wp.7 70M) just below the summit, which is reached by following the red and blue waymarks up to the right.

The descent is made by the southerly path, which skitters down quite steeply at first. Following the clearer traces wherever the path appears to splinter, we eventually reach level ground and a cairnmarked Y-junction on the edge of a

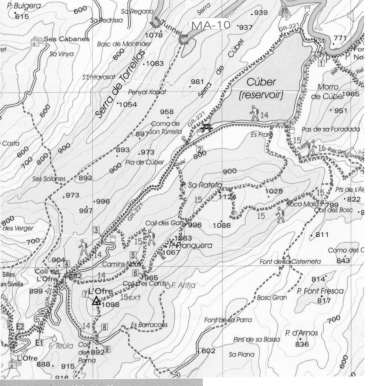

stand of mature pine (Wp.8 84M). Taking the fork to the right, we descend alongside a wall to join a broad dirt track at the **Coll d'en Poma** (Wp.9 87M). A faint way directly in front of us marks the start of the descent to **Pas de na Maria** and is worth taking for a few metres to see the dilapidated remains of a hugely improbable sightseers' telescope.

Sightseen, we take the dirt track to the northwest, enjoying an agreeable stroll through the woods before rejoining the main Ofre track just below the **Coll de l'Ofre** (Wp.4 101M). To return to the starting point we simply retrace our steps to the reservoir, then follow the opposite shoreline to the one taken earlier.

For the extension to **Sóller**, we follow the GR as it drops down to the southwest, crossing the dirt track before descending steadily to a T-junction (Wp.E1 15M from **Coll de l'Ofre**). Turning right, then left when we rejoin the dirt track, we pass another telescope and turn right on a clearly signposted path when the track approaches the **Ofre** farmhouse (Wp.E2 25M). 100 metres later, we go through a gate and embark on an extraordinary descent along the **Es Barranc** donkey trail.

You really oughtn't to be reading a book at this stage, but to give you an idea of what to expect, the trail descends alongside the **Biniaraix** torrent before levelling out above cliff tops, from where we have superb views down to **Sóller** and the sea. Leaving the **Ofre** estate by a second gate, we resume our descent below towering cliffs streaked with water stains. We cross the torrent three times, after which it dries out and we continue our steady descent through shady, green terraces. After a fourth crossing, a very gentle climb brings us onto a dirt track leading into **Biniaraix** village beside the old *lavadero* (Wp.E3 85M).

We can either return to **Sóller** via the road (the conventional and quickest end to this itinerary), or (recommended) follow the more roundabout GR route via **Binibassi**, which is more peaceful and picturesque. From the *lavadero* (Wp.BS01), we take **Carrer de Sant Josep** into **Biniaraix** then turn right after 75 metres (the only junction without a sign or waypost) onto **Carrer de Santa Catarina** (Wp.BS02). Thereafter, wayposts guide us onto a cobbled trail that becomes a narrow lane leading to the **Fornalutx** road (Wp.BS03 10M from the *lavadero*). Turning left then right 50 metres later, we follow the **Camí de Binibassi** all the way back to **Sóller**, mainly on quiet lanes but descending from the hamlet of **Binibassi** on an old cobbled path. The cam debouches on the MA2122 (Wp.BS04) 150 metres from **Sóller** football ground (Wp.BS05 35M from the *lavadero*).

15 SA RATETA

At first glance, **Sa Rateta**, the scruffy rock south of the **Cúber Reservoir**, is as mousy as its name suggests, a rather furtive rise with no distinguishing crown and no very apparent way to the top. Yet it's one of my favourite little mountains in Mallorca, a wonderfully wild and isolated spot with commanding views of the more majestic summits surrounding it, so it was a pleasure to return for this revised version of our original walk.

In earlier editions of this book, we climbed **Rateta** via the scree gully on its northern face, the route of which GPS users can see on the PNF CD. In the new version, for which I am indebted to a reader (anonymous, I'm afraid, the name got detached from the information, but you know who you are thank you!), we descend into the **Torrent d'Almedra** (as per Walk 16), then climb **Rateta** via the **Coll d'es Bosc** to the south, an approach that opens up an interesting perspective on the **Comasema** and **Sólleric** estates.

N.B. If you only have time for one walk up here, it would be logical to extend the present itinerary to include the ascent of **Ofre** described in Walk 14 (Wps. 69 and 42)

The itinerary is only recommended for experienced walkers, as it traverses rough, frequently pathless terrain.

4   3½ H   10.5 km   450m 450m   0

Access: by car or bus
Stroll: as per Walk 14
Extension: **L'Ofre** (see Walk 14)

Sa Rateta & Ofre from the MA10

From the Cúber parking area (Wp.1 0M), we take the tarmac track alongside the reservoir then turn left just before the dam (Wp.2 11M) on a rough track that soon dwindles to a trail climbing across a rise, where the **Torrent d'Almedra** gorge opens out before us. On the far side of the torrent, we can see an interred aquifer rising toward a bulging cliff on the right, which is where the present itinerary diverges from Walk 16.

After dropping down to cross the torrent, we climb to the cliff, immediately below which cairns and the word 'Rateta' daubed in red on the concrete wall indicate where our path climbs to the right (Wp.3 26M). Though not visible from below, the path almost immediately becomes clear, long cobbled sections zigzagging up for 50 metres, after which the gradient eases. Following cairns and occasional red dots, we cross a *sitja*, 20 metres after which there is a waymarked fork (Wp.4 33M).

on the donkey trail

Ignoring the branch to the right, we maintain direction (S), climbing across sheets of rock and patches of path to the **Coll d'es Bosc**, where green painted letters on the right indicate the ongoing route for **Rateta** (Wp.5 41M).

At first, for anyone with an affinity for paths, the prospect is not promising, but if you look up toward the folds of rock, you will see the sloping margins of a retaining wall defining a snow gatherers' donkey trail. Following the cairnmarked route, we climb across the rocks to join the donkey trail just above a tailored chicane (Wp.6 50M).

We now simply follow the cobbled trail and the route indicated by cairns when the trail becomes obscure, pausing to enjoy fine views of the **Alar** and **Alcaldena** summits to the south. Following a steady climb, the donkey trail swings right (Wp.7) on a slightly obscure stretch before resuming its westerly course. After traversing an area of bare rock (Wp.8 58M), we wade through a shallow swale of *carritx* to reach the foot of the last tailored stretch (Wp.9

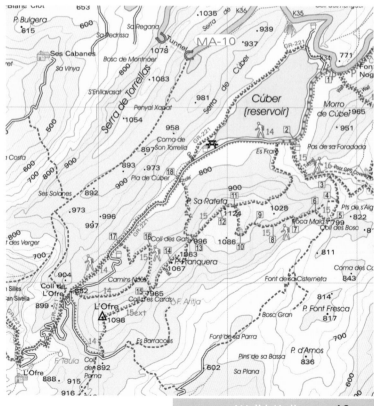

71M), which leads us to the roofless ruin of a snow gatherers' cabin (Wp.10 75M) and the end of anything very pathlike.

admiring the views

Various cairn-marked routes climb to the ridge from here, the clearest heading due north to reach the first of several small summits (Wp.11 80M). Bearing left across sheets of limestone, we traverse the main summit, staying on the nearside of the ridge and heading in a southwesterly direction until a clear patch of path (Wp.12 85M) indicates where we veer further left, away from the ridge, to follow a cairnmarked route down to the **Coll d'es Gats** (Wp.13 98M).

If you need an escape route, it is possible to cross the wall here and follow very faint sheep trail marked with cairns down to the north, into the **Ofr** valley. The cairns disappear after 150 metres and the trail splinters into confusing web of ways, but winding through the carritx in a norther direction and aiming to pass to the right of the stand of pine at the bottom the slope, you will come to a broken down fence punctured with numerou rambler-sized holes (Wp.18). The descent takes about 15 minutes and join the main track a little over half an hour from the start. NOTE: a solitary cair at the bottom suggests the 'approved' descent is straight down the slope in northwesterly direction, but a traverse is gentler on the knees.

To continue along the ridge from **Coll d'es Gats**, we stay on the near side the wall and bear left at the southwestern end of the coll to follow a fain cairn-marked way skirting behind the obvious (very obvious!) crag blockin direct progress. Natural 'steps' in the rock bring us back onto the ridge, whe we bear left and, staying well back from the cliffs, climb to the sma **Franquera** summits (Wp.14 118M). Our next objective is a wall, only th head of which is visible at first, making it look like a cabin. Crossing the wa 15 metres from its upper end, we descend (SW) along a steep, stony way t reach the **Coll d'es Cards** (Wp.15 133M). Which is where we intersect wit Walk 14.

To return to **Cúber**, we head north, crossing a broken wall to take a clear pat down to a Y-junction. Continuing straight on (the right hand branch), we be right at the next metal pylon and descend steadily through the pine, passin occasional cairns before emerging at a large *sitja* (Wp.16 143M). Bearing le (SW) on a broad trail, we descend to a trickling stream and large trough besid a stand of poplars. Taking the fainter of the two cow paths on the eastern sid of the stream, we meander down, crossing a tangle of paths, half-paths an runoff channels, to emerge on the **Ofre** dirt track opposite a small by (Wp.17 158M). Turning right, we follow the dirt track back to **Cúber** returning to the start either via the GR on the northern side of the reservoir via the tarmac track to the south.

?

This adventurous excursion takes us through five rough tunnels piping water down from the **Cúber** reservoir, visits Mallorca's first manned and still most popular refuge, and circles the **Tossals Verds** massif along shady charcoal-burning paths. It is possible to cross all except the second tunnel without a torch (if you don't mind not seeing where you put your feet), but not recommended. During the descent, you will see painted signs announcing a toll for the privilege of crossing the **Solleric** estate. I have not heard of anyone actually being asked to pay.

| 4 | 4 H | 13 km | 450m / 450m | ↻ | 4 *** |

*** The refuge (open all year) and has dormitory accommodation for 30. Book even for eating, as it's popular with large parties (Tel: 971 182027).

Access: by car and bus. An alternative access to this route is via the refuge service road from the south (see Tour & Trail map). The last 2.5km open to cars are a bit pot-holey, but thereafter it's an attractive stroll through the gorge. The other advantage is that parking here is less risky than at the top end, which is notorious for car break-ins.

Starting from the **Área Recreative de Sa Font des Noguera** at km33.8 of the MA-10 (Wp.1 0M), we cross the stile at the western end of the car-park and follow the GR to **Cúber**, where we take the tarmac track along the southern side of the reservoir. When the tarmac track swings right to cross the dam wall (Wp.2 10M), we bear left on a dirt track. The track soon narrows to a walking trail descending steeply on loose stones and passing a tunnel with a concrete pipe running through it – this is NOT one of our tunnels. Ten minutes from the dam wall we cross a torrent, then follow the course of the large, occasionally interred concrete water-pipe, along an easy dirt path. A steady then gentle climb brings us through a cutting onto a small plateau littered with sections of discarded piping.

Descending from the plateau, gently at first then more steeply along a rough, rock strewn path, we come to the first of the tunnels (on our right), dubbed 'Sollerich Paso', (Wp.3 40M).

The valley above the tunnels

The first tunnel is easy, the second less so: you can't see the exit, the ground's rough, it dips down at the end, and you have to be careful not to clout your head on the roof. After a much longer descent, we come to the third tunnel, which has a low entrance, but is in fact easier than the first two with a well beaten path and large window halfway along. The fourth is little more than an archway, the fifth and last has been roughly gated. Leaving the fifth tunnel (Wp.4 65M) we bear right on a rough track (direction

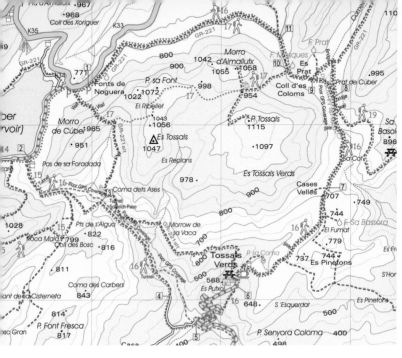

'Sals'). After ten minutes, we ignore a branch on the right and continue on the main track for a steady descent to a large metal gate and ladder-stile leading to a small wooden bridge (Wp.5 80M).

Crossing the bridge, we join the tarmac lane from **Almedrà**. After climbing up the lane for ten minutes, we bear right at a signpost indicating the refuge is a further ten minutes away, and follow a stony trail climbing steeply across the terraces. We rejoin the lane shortly before the refuge gates (Wp.6 100M), from where we have good views of the **Alcaldena** and **Alaró** mountains to the south-west. To the left of the main refuge building, we take the signposted path on the right for 'Cases Velles 35M / Font des Noguera 2H', passing through a gate and climbing across terraces. A steady then gentle climb with fine views of the terraced valley below **Cases Velles**, passes first a large pine tree (to our left), **El Fumat**, reputedly the largest of its kind in the region, then a signposted path on the right for **Mancor des Valles** (not recommended). A path to the left (Wp.7 140M) a few metres before a GR waypost, leads to the terraces below **Cases Velles**, where there are innumerable fine picnic spots.

Continuing along the main path, we circle **Tossals Verds**, passing the celebrated **Canaleta de Massanella** (see Walk 19), before crossing and re-crossing the stream just below it (Wp.8 200M). A gentle climb brings us past the turning for **Massanella** and **Lluc**, signposted 'Font d'es Prat' (Wp.9 205M) and the branch to **Puig Tossals Verds** (Wp.10 210M). We then cross **Coll d'es Colloms** for a steady descent along a roughly cobbled trail down to a gate and a bridge over the new concrete *canaleta* (Wp.11 225M). Bearing left, we walk alongside the *canaleta* (doubtless on a hot day wishing we were IN it) back to our starting point in a little over thirty minutes.

17 TWIN PEAKS AND ONE MAD MALLORCAN LOOP

The **Tossals Verds Circuit** is well known, yet hardly anybody ventures up the massif itself, which is puzzling because it's an easy climb to a wonderful little wilderness. The **Twin Peaks** are **Puig de Tossals Verds** and **Morro d'Almallutx**. Both involve rough pathless walking, but neither are difficult and the first could be done by a moderately fit family. The loop is something else. Few obstacles daunt your average Mallorcan rambler and it sometimes seems as if, having established perfectly feasible, roundabout routes, locals look at the map, draw a straight line and say, 'Let's do it <u>that</u> way', regardless of what lies in between. The loop via **Es Ribellet** is far from being a straight line, but the mentality is the same. It's horrendous: very rough, very gruelling, very steep, very pathless! It was indicated to me by a young Mallorcan family, who seemed to think it suitable for children. Frankly, it's not suitable for most adults, let alone children. So why include it? Simply because I know there are people out there for whom the single word 'horrendous' will be enough to have them strapping on their boots and booking their tickets. Be warned though, it is only for very experienced walkers. Everybody else should settle for one of the Short Versions. Finally, given that this is wild, little visited terrain, please observe the basic and commonly ignored rules: Don't walk alone; Do tell someone where you're going. NOTE: **Coll d'es Colloms** is at Wp.3, <u>not</u> Wp.5 where most maps place it.

| 5* | 4-4½H* | 9 km | 725m ***725m | ↻ | 0 |

*   Short Versions **(a)** & **(b)** 4
*** Short Version **(a)** 300 metres **(b)** 375 metres

> ### Short Versions
> (a) **Morro d'Almallutx** returning via **Coll d'es Colloms** 3h
> (b) **Puig Tossals Verds** returning via **Coll d'es Colloms** 3½h

Access: by car or bus (seasonal timetable)

Starting just below **Font des Noguera Área Recreativa**, we take the GR-221 east, signposted 'Font d'es Prat/Refugi des Tossals Verds' (Wp.1 0M), and follow the open concrete *canaleta* until it swings round into the **Almallutx** valley, where we cross the *canaleta* via a broad concrete ramp (the fourth) (Wp.2 30M).

Morro d'Almallutx & Puig de sa Font

We then go through a wooden gate and climb steadily through the oak wood along a partially stepped charcoal-burners' trail that levels out on the **Coll d'es Colloms**, from where we can see our **Twin Peaks** up to the right. 30 metres after the *coll*, a signpost indicates our branch on the right (Wp.3 40M).

Walk 17 waypoint 3

Following a delightful sun-dappled path strewn with dead oak leaves (SSW), we pass (after 200 metres) the first of several old pink waymarks, after which the climb gradually gets steeper and the cairns larger.

Bearing left at a 'Caça Controlada' signpost (Wp.4 50M), we cross the bed of a watercourse, taking care to follow the cairns and waymarks, and gradually climb away from the **Morro d'Almallutx** before emerging from the oak wood behind a large pinnacle. A final brief climb along a clear, eroded path brings us through a gap in a wall (Wp.5 60M) onto the misnamed *coll* between our **Twin Peaks**. On the far side of the *coll* there is a large snowpit. We now have a choice of routes. **Tossals Verds** is the easier, gentler and less hazardous climb, despite being slightly higher, while **Morro d'Almallutx** is a rougher, wilder place, better suited to those with a passion for getting off the beaten track - though that's a passion that will be utterly sated if you do the full circuit! N.B. All subsequent timings assume climbing both peaks, though one will probably be enough for most people.

For the Morro d'Almallutx
We bear right to the ruins of the snow-gatherers' cabin, behind which a cairn marks the start of the ascent up a shallow gully. At the top of the gully, we bear left for 10 metres before swinging back to resume our northerly direction, picking our way over the rocks and passing occasional cairns indicating a rough line to the top (Wp.6 80M), where the 'Grup Es Voltors' left their mark in 1994. Taking particular care on the sharp rocks at the top, we return to Wp.5 via the same route.

For Puig d'es Tossals Verds
We bear left just before the snowpit on the *coll*, and climb along a reasonably clear way marked with cairns, heading for the rocky outcrop to the right of the *puig* (SSW). A steady climb with fine views of **Puig Major** leads to a large cairn (Wp.7 110M) 50 metres behind the guiding outcrop, in full view of the **Alaró** and **Alcaldena** 'sugar loaf' mountains. Bearing left, we follow the clear, cairn-marked way (NE) up to the **Tossals Verds** trig point (Wp.8 120M). We return to Wp.5 via the same route.

This is probably enough mountain for most people and I recommend returning to **Font d'es Noguera via Coll d'es Colloms**. If you feel like an adventure though, head west. But remember: this is pathless country with steep descents and only sporadic cairns to help us on our way.

For the full circuit
We head into the valley to the west of the snowpit and follow the cairn marked route, meandering through the *carritx* then dipping down to pass below two huge fingers of rock poking out from the northern ridge (Wp.9 145M [7M from the *coll*]). Bearing right (NW), we follow cairns up to a depression in the ridge to the right of a small top flanked by a pinnacle of rock.

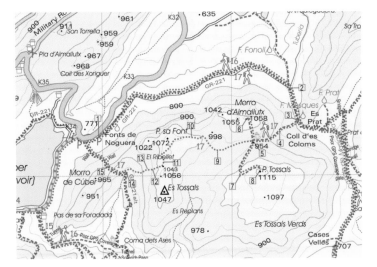

Turning towards the pinnacle, we skirt the first small top (SW) to cross onto a second depression in the ridge with superb views over **Gorg Blau** (Wp.10 155M).

We now follow the ridge (W) staying a little way behind the crest and passing very occasional cairns. Staying below the jagged limestone running up to **Puig de sa Font** (barely distinguishable from the rest of the ridge), we pick our way through *carritx* (SW) toward two distinct small tops on our left (S), the second of which, **Es Tossals**, has a large, clearly visible cairn on top. Just before the first of these two tops, with the **Cúber** reservoir visible to the north-west, a cairn (Wp.11 175M) marks the start of our first <u>very rough</u> descent. If you look to the right, you'll see a wall along a narrow ridge with a path snaking up to the wall from the south. This path is our objective.

There's no approved way down to this path, only a steep scree slope, and it's basically a question of picking your way down as best you can. Walking poles may be useful, otherwise you have to grab the *carritx* and whatever comes to hand to steady yourself on the steeper sections. It's slightly easier if you hug the rocks on the left until about 50 metres before they end in a large knoll. From here, we bear right, away from the rocks to cut across into the main channel of scree, where we find another cairn (Wp.12 190M). We now take maximum advantage of every potential zigzag, passing two more cairns on a long chute of debris (Wp.13 200M) and aiming for the obvious v-shaped defile at the bottom of the slope. Finally, with considerable relief, we lever ourselves down the defile and cross the remaining 75 metres of scrub and rock to join the path (Wp.14 210M) above the orange and white wreck of a light aircraft, visible through much of the descent.

Bearing right, we climb along the stony path to a gap in the wall on the ridge (Wp.15 220M). Winding through the rocks on the far side of the wall, we soon see the **Font des Noguera Área Recreativa** below us. Heading towards **Cúber** (NW) we pick our way through the *carritx* to a second wall, where a very rough path descends steeply to the GR-221 between the **Cúber** and **Font d'es Noguera** parking areas in a little under twenty minutes.

Very long, very high, very tough. So what's the attraction? Basically that - it's very long, very high and very tough. This is challenge time, the macho end of walking, for the sort of people who gaze at towering cliffs and say to themselves, 'I want to be up there'. If you have to ask yourself 'Can I do it?', the answer is probably no. Nonetheless, the reasons for trying aren't all childish. It is a very satisfying route, the views are unparalleled, and the ridge, which dominates the **Sóller** valley, is bound to draw the walker's eye as it's such an obvious and, in many ways, perfect loop. But I can't emphasise enough, this is <u>very tough</u> walking. Most walkers will have an idea what a 1000 metre climb entails. The difference here is that the tough walking only begins <u>after</u> you've done the climbing. Once on top, you've got four kilometres of virtually pathless terrain, hopping across fissured slabs of limestone and *carritx* covered boulders. Every step of the way is a potential twisted ankle and, since the only company you'll find on top are eagles and vultures, it's essential that you don't go alone. Thanks to the cluster of antennae above **Sa Serra**, there is some mobile phone coverage, but as ever in the mountains, this should not be relied on. And do not venture up here in poor conditions. Trackless limestone, high cliffs, deep potholes and dense cloud cover are not a happy combination. Bear in mind that conditions at this altitude and proximity to the sea can change rapidly. Twenty minutes after we descended from the ridge under clear, blue skies, it was submerged in cloud! If you're still reading, if there's a fervid gleam in your eye, if your hands are trembling and your legs twitching with excitement, then this might be the walk for you. But do observe all the usual precautions, and take plenty of food and a <u>minimum</u> of two litres water per person. The route is waymarked with red dots and cairns till Wp.8, after which we're on our own, except for a few cairns along the ridge.

* - though distance and the roughness of the terrain send it off the scale.
** Timing is exact, but the rough terrain and pathfinding problems mean this is a more approximate guide than usual. Allow 10 h including rest-stops etc..

Short Versions & Strolls
Given the steep climb, there's little here that could be called a 'stroll', but Wps.2, 3, 4, & 6 are pleasant picnic spots and would serve as natural objectives for linear walks. Those who don't fancy the pathless ridge but want comparable views can continue along the dirt track from Wp.9 to the private **Jovenolles** refuge (see map) some twenty-five minutes to the east (visible from the **Sa Serra** farm) and return the same way.

Access: on foot from **Sóller**

From **Sóller**'s central *plaza*, we take **Carrer de Joan Baptista Ensenyat** to the left of the church. Turning first left (**Carrer de Sant Jaume**) then first right brings us into the short **Carrer de Sant Nicolau** (signposted 'Cementiri'). We turn left at the end of **Carrer de Sant Nicolau**, then right 15 metres later into **Carrer de Pau Noguera**, which we follow to the cemetery

.(Wp.1 10M). Immediately after the cemetery, we take the narrow path climbing between the torrent and **Cami de Can Petra**, crossing the road 150-metres later and continuing on cobbled stairs marked with old red dots. The stairs climb steeply before winding through a chicane and leading into a partially cobbled path zigzagging up across abandoned terraces and passing a ruined cabin.

After climbing steadily, the path levels out briefly (Wp.2 30M) and we bear left, heading for a second ruin 15 metres away, where we climb onto a path <u>behind</u> the ruin. Climbing steadily then more steeply, we cross a second level stretch of about 50 metres, at the end of which we branch left to continue climbing, passing a partially restored cabin, **Can Selles** (Wp.3 45M), and another cabin where someone has etched Sóller's coat of arms into a rock (Wp.4 60M). After a third level stretch, from where we can glimpse the roundabout at the southern end of the **Sóller** by-pass, we come to the upper limit of the terracing. Entering a mixed pine and oak wood, the path swings left, zigzagging steeply up beside a stone wall. The route's not always clear, but it's well waymarked with red dots and, in spring, studded with tiny cyclamen. After a shady climb between pine, oak and tumbledown outcrops of limestone, we pass through a wall gateway (Wp.5 80M) where we bear left to continue zigzagging up through the woods (SSW).

After emerging on a level, less densely wooded, *carritx* covered ridge overlooking the steeply scarped **Rafel de Gaspar** valley on our left (E), we go through another wall gateway, beyond which we must take particular care following the waymarks through the *carritx*. 100 metres after the wall, we bear right, into the woods rather than left towards **Es Rafel**, staying more or less on the level for 50 metres before cairns indicate a path to the left. The path winds onto a natural 'terrace', climbing slightly (WSW) before swinging left to cross a dead pine with two cairns perched on the trunk. Following the cairns and waymarks, we climb steeply, sometimes on a vague path, sometimes on exposed rock, passing above a small *sitja* (Wp.6 105M).

After climbing steeply on a long limestone slope, the path bears back towards **Es Rafel** (SE), where we ignore a large cairn to the left (Wp.7 110M) and continue climbing. 50 metres later, we come onto another limestone shelf, where some cairns appear to lead us off to the left, but we in fact carry on over the rocks for our first sight of the radio masts above **Sa Serra** (115M).

The path is unclear, but aiming for the tall, solitary, central antenna, we soon pick up cairns and waymarks, guiding us along what is in effect a huge spur, from where we have fine views of **Puig Major** and the **Teix Massif**. The antennae disappear behind a succession of low crags separating us from the **Sa Serra** farmhouse. Using a couple of short retaining walls, we climb behind the first crag before skirting to the left of the second and third crags. Cairns and red waymarks guide us over the final rocks, gradually

... fine views of Puig Major ...

bringing the antennae back into partial then, at a tall cairn on a small plateau (Wp.8 135M), full view. At the lowest point on the ridge, just left of the antennae, we can see Wp.10, an unnamed *coll* pricked with fencing posts.

Aiming for a second large cairn 75 metres to the south then bearing left toward two smaller cairns, we pick up an old cow path on the left of the last rocky outcrop before the farm. Going through a gateway formed by the remains of an old fence and wall, we bear right (SW) to climb toward a comparatively large oak tree with distinctively tangled branches. Maintaining direction on a naturally 'cobbled' route, we come into view of the farm buildings, where the waymarks end. Going to the left of the farm, we find a clear path leading to the farm's access track (Wp.9 150M), from where we can see the roof of the **Jovenolles** refuge in the distance.

We turn left and follow the dirt track past a large pine to cross the dry torrent running down from the *coll*, immediately after which, we turn right, leaving the track and climbing a faint stony path for 50 metres to join the remains of an old cart track (visible as we approach the pine tree, but not from where we leave the main track) carpeted with euphorbia. The cart track climbs steadily (E) before doubling back towards the antennae (SW), re-crossing the dry torrent and climbing to peter out at an old snow-pit, 50 metres below the antennae. 5 metres above the pit, a tiny sheep path heads toward a solitary pine tree just below the *coll*. The path soon disappears, but maintaining direction (SE), we climb to the pine tree, from where it's an easy 30 metre scramble up to the *coll* (Wp.10 180M) and over the low fence onto the ridge.

Some walkers turn left here, directly onto the first part of the ridge. This is both undesirable and indescribable. The rocks are so steep, the fissures so deep, the *carritx* covered boulders so treacherous, it's like dancing on needles, and a few hundred metres can mean forty minutes of blood, sweat and tears (not necessarily in that order). <u>From the *coll*, descend directly to the dirt track 50 metres below the southern side of the ridge</u>. This seems crazy after all the climbing, but I assure you, it's not. The track is fenced off, but never mind - just get over, under or through that fence, as if your life depended on it (it doesn't quite, but after ten minutes dancing on the needles, you may well believe it does). We made the mistake of trying the full ridge route before giving it up as a bad job (sweat and tears, no blood) and descending to the dirt track, so the timing between Wps.10 & 11 is estimated.

Once past the fence, turn left. After about 500 metres, the dirt track dips down then climbs steeply toward the westernmost rocks (clearly visible) flanking the **Alfàbia** peak. Going through a gap in the fence (Wp.11 195M), we pass a broad platform and catch sight again of the **Jovenolles** refuge below us, after which the track dwindles to a stony path crossing a rockspill to climb behind the first outcrop of rocks on the main ridge. The 'path' is really just a succession of ways, climbing steeply and winding through the *carritx*, but staying just behind the ridge and maintaining a generally easterly direction, we eventually see to our left the tall white trig point of the **Alfàbia** summit (Wp.12 215M), an easy 20 metre scramble for a birds-eye view of the **Sóller** plain, the **Orient** valley, and the entire **Tramuntana**.

Returning to the 'path' and bearing left (E), we pass that welcome harbinger of civilisation, a cairn! But don't get too excited. We're now entering virtually pathless terrain and the cairns are minimal. Passing between the summit and the next mini-ridge, we traverse the northern side of the ridge before climbing to a tiny pass beside a second small top (Wp.13 225M). We now skirt the southern side of the mini-ridge, staying on the rock, till the cairns take us across rough, virtually pathless terrain down to a broad *coll*, from where we can see **Orient** village and the white sanctuary within **Castell d'Alaró**.

Still following the cairns, we climb a slight rise for our first sight of the **Cúber Reservoir**. Fifty metres beyond the rise, we cross a wall beside a large cairn at what appears to be its northern tip (Wp.14 240M). In fact, the wall continues on the far side. Bearing left, we follow the cairns on a route parallel to the wall, descending into a shallow depression dotted with oak. The occasional cairns are hidden in the trees here and are harder to spot, but maintaining direction (NE) and running parallel to the wall till it ends, we eventually climb out of the wooded depression toward a large cairn.

Cairns are scarce here, but continuing on rough limestone debris, we aim between **Puig Major** and a distinct upright stone marking a small top slightly to the left. The debris gives way to ridges and slanting sheets of rock as we skirt the head of a shallow gully on our left, after which we can climb to the upright stone (Wp.15 255M) where we get our first glimpse (to the right, in line with **Puig Major**) of the **Es Cornadors** refuge.

Alfábia cliffs from Sementer Gran

Returning to the shallow depression behind the upright stone and keeping the next small peak ('Small Peak X') to our left (take care, there is at least one deep pothole here), we see the **Cúber Reservoir** more clearly again, and pick our way with infinite patience across the increasingly fractured and treacherous rockscape, <u>heading all the time for **Puig Major**</u> (no cairns here). 200 metres after **Small Peak X**, we come to another wall, which we cross beside a rusted black and white private hunting sign (Wp.16 270M).

The reservoir disappears from sight again and we continue our painstaking progress across the limestone and *carritx*, staying about 30 metres behind the cliffs, still heading for **Puig Major**, and passing the very occasional cairn - well, one actually!

We now have to pass to the <u>left</u> of **Sementer Gran**, the last summit on the ridge. **Cúber** comes back into view as well as the dirt track descending to the **Ofre** farm, at which point we start bearing left towards **Sementer Gran**, just before which we can see **Ofre** farm itself.

Skirting to the left of the peak with impressive views of the cliffs behind us, we come back into sight of the **Es Cornadors** refuge where we can see that ineffable luxury, a real path!

First though we have to follow the rough cairn marked way down to the junction of paths (left up to the refuge and the *mirador*, right down to **Sóller**) at the *coll* 50 metres below the refuge, where there is a concrete marker post (Wp.17 295M). Given that we've probably had more than enough views and climbs for the day, we turn right for **Sóller**.

We now really stretch our legs out on the well-made path zigzagging down to the **Barranc de Biniaraix**. Don't stretch your legs out too far, though - the gravel is loose and accidents tend to happen in the stupidest places. Ignore all branch paths and stick to the main path, finally fording (the bridge has been swept away) the torrent (Wp.18 320M). From here we have a straightforward seventy-minute descent along the classic **Es Barranc** cobbled trail following the GR221. For an outline of the route, see Walk 14.

Famously constructed by a Mallorcan pig farmer after the great engineers of the age said it wasn't possible, the **Canaleta de Massanella** is an eighteenth century *aquifer* that is still in use today, bringing water down from the **Font des Prat** to **Mancor del Valle**. The fact that the professionals baulked at building in such inhospitable terrain may explain why the canaleta has often been regarded as altogether too hairy by many walkers, myself not excluded, who fear they'll end up on all fours, peering over the precipice, wondering whether stampcollecting wouldn't be a wiser pastime. In fact, the dangers are often exaggerated. They are real and should not be dismissed out of hand, but it's a lot less vertiginous than many aquifers I've walked (or, in one instance, crawled) and described in other publications, and so long as you have a reasonable head for heights and are careful where you put your feet, the risk is not great. The rewards, however, in terms of isolation, views, and the sheer thrill of it all cannot be exaggerated, and even those who don't want to venture onto the *canaleta* should take the time to do the short version, which is a delight in itself. Given the nature of the walk, it is not recommended when the *canaleta* is wet.

Though adequate, GPS reception is not consistent either in the woods or in the lee of the cliffs.

Short Version: to Wp.7 then down onto the bridge to loop back to Wp.4.
Extension: **Mancor del Valle** (see text)

Our itinerary starts (as per Walk 17) from below the **Font des Noguer Área Recreativa** on the GR221, signposted 'Font d'es Prat, Refugi des Tossals Verds' (Wp.1 0M).

an 'easy' stretch

We begin with a pleasant stroll alongside a modern, concrete *canaleta*, enjoying fine views over **Gorg Blau** and passing three concrete ramps bridging the *aquifer*. After nearly two and a half kilometres, we cross the aquifer via the fourth ramp (Wp.2 32M).

Still following the GR, we climb via a partially cobbled trail to the **Coll d'es Coloms**, where Walk 17 branches off to the right (Wp.3 39M). 300 metres later, after a gentle descent, we turn left for 'Font d'es Prat' (Wp.4 47M). Ignoring a fork on the left 50 metres later (Wp.5), we stay on the GR until it reaches a signposted junction immediately south of **Font d'es Prat**, where we can already see the partially interred head of the old *canaleta* (Wp.6 53M).

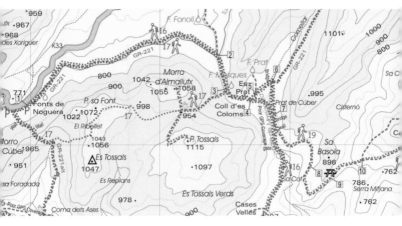

We leave the GR at this juncture, crossing the small stone bridge immediately after the signpost and bearing right to follow a faint trodden way parallel to the stream. After passing a large limekiln 100 metres later, the path becomes clearer, winding through lovely woodland before joining the *canaleta* proper at two metal hatches (Wp.7 57M).

Easy strolling continues as the *canaleta* passes above a wooden footbridge (an alternative approach and the turning point for the Short Version), but we soon cross a wall, after which we reach the first vertiginous bit, a delicately arched aqueduct, a little under a metre wide, where you may find yourself (I know I did) proceeding with the concentrated determination of a two year old who is still a little unsteady on his feet.

Thereafter, things get easier again, a rough, rocky slope dotted with trees slanting away below us as we pass a *sitja*, from where we can see a short tunnel on the far side of the valley where the *canaleta* pierces an outcrop of rock.

at the tunnel

After the first of several taps set into the wall, the *canaleta* swings right, passing an off-path cairn-marked descent to the right (Wp.8 76M), 130 metres after which, we go through the tunnel again, slightly vertiginous as we have to step out onto a ledge over a ten metre drop.

At the next bend, wonderful views open out to the south and the drop gets appreciably greater as the *canaleta* starts to descend slightly, passing a fifteen metre stretch which was the only place where I developed a 'Let's hug!' affinity for the rockface. We then pass above a lovely *sitja* (Wp.9 88M), which is ideal for a picnic spot and where I recommend most people stop unless you want to enjoy some fine views of **Puig de Massanella** (Walk 27) and **Puig n'Ali** (Walk 46) or intend doing the extension.

a 'less easy' stretch

Shortly after the picnic *sitja*, the trees close in around us and the *canaleta* descends in a straight line through the woods to a very slight right hand bend where large cairns mark a path descending to the left (Wp.10 93M).

In the unlikely event that you can arrange to be dropped off at the top and picked up at the bottom, this would be a pleasant extension. The path on the left zigzags down through the woods to reach an attractive *casa forestal* half an hour later. Simple bear right and follow the dirt track down the valley to reach the **Son Catlar** restaurant on the Mancor-Caimari road in another half hour.

Those of you who don't have the luxury of a lift at the end of the walk but who want to see some fine views of **Massanella** and the surrounding summits can continue along the *canaleta* for another 600 metres as it descends ever more steeply through the woods (you'll have to duck under overhanging branches and skirt two stretches where low branches and fallen trees block the path) until it curves below cliffs to cross a wall, where it gets even steeper and eventually dangerous (Wp.11 108M).

We return via the same route, with the option of forking left 100 metres after the wall north of the aqueduct (Wp.12 166M) to cross the **Torrent des Prat** by the wooden bridge seen earlier, beyond which a clear trail feeds into the GR and brings us back to Wp.4 (172M).

This tiny but testing little walk is ideal at the end of the day or for motorists who've descended the tortuous **Sa Calobra** road (an extraordinary trip in itself), but don't have much time. The walk itself is unremarkable, but the **Mola de Tuent** *torre*, chapel and customs hut, are exceptional, beautifully restored and with superb views in all directions.

Access: by car – or on foot if staying in **Sa Calobra** or **Cala Tuent**.

We start from the car-park beside **Sant Llorenç** 'church' (a chapel in all but name) on the *coll* above **Cala Tuent** (Wp.1 0M). Behind the house attached to the chapel we take a gravelly path, climbing steeply to the small cliffs north of the *coll*. Shortly before the wall at the top of these cliffs, we pass a vertiginous stretch where a steel cable has been set in the rock (well-set at the time of writing, but test it before trusting your weight to it). N.B. If you find this passage at the limit of the tolerable on the way up, don't insist and simply turn back, as it's more alarming in descent. If you do insist and find yourselves in difficulty on the way back, descend with your back to the drop, which is a lot less hypnotic when you're not looking at it!

Beyond the wall above this cable we come onto a cistus-covered slope from where we already have fine views back towards **Puig Mayor**. Winding through dense cistus interspersed with the odd clump of *carritx* and *pistacia*, we climb steadily (NNE) on a faint, occasionally slightly confusing path. The path seems to end in a patch of barer ground just below the second outcrop of rocks (Wp.2 20M), but orienting ourselves by a small retaining wall, we maintain our general direction (N) winding through the cistus. Bearing left (SW) at a second cairn then right (NW) 50 metres later, we climb through waist high cistus, thyme, *carritx* and *pistacia* before emerging within sight of the **La Mola** buildings (Wp.3 25M). The path remains crazily overgrown and from a distance is invisible, but heading for the *torre*, the way clarifies itself as we progress. Passing just left of twin pines and ignoring the apparently clearer way through the *carritx* patch on our left, we continue wading through cistus (now chest deep), finally climbing up between the chapel and customs hut, thirty metres west of the tower (Wp.4 35M).

La Mola

The views are stunning, but even more stunning is the quality of the restoration work in this inaccessible site. The buildings are locked, but benches and a few grassy patches in the shade of trees make ideal picnic spots. Return by the same route.

21 CALA TUENT - SA COSTERA - CALA TUENT

Easy walking along a lovely corniche path to the superbly situated house at **Sa Costera**, with an optional excursion to the **Fábrica de Luz** hydro-electric generating station. Traditionally part of the **Ses Barques/Sa Calobra** route, returning by boat.

3	3H *	10 km	400m ** 400m	3 ***

*   + 35M for the extension and at least an hour for exploring and picnicking
**   + 150 metres for the extension
*** in **Cala Tuent**

Short Version	**Stroll**	**Extension**
To La Fábrica and back (see text)	(a) bear right at Wp. 2 on the **Tuent/Es Vergeret** path back to the restaurant. (b) to the **Coll de ne Pollo**.	**La Fábrica** (see text).

Access: by car or boat.

We start from the **Cala Tuent Es Vergeret Bar/Restaurante** on a dirt track between **C'an Boy** and the restaurant gates, signposted 'Sa Costera, Fornalutx, Sóller' (Wp.1 0M). After 100 metres, we pass a branch track and turn right on a signposted partially cobbled path. Climbing through the woods, we come to a third signpost (Wp.2 7M) below a broad dirt track, which we follow till it ends 75 metres later.

Cala Tuent

Recovering the cobbled trail, we climb to another dirt track in front of a large, tastefully restored farmhouse, where we turn right. When the track bears left 50 metres later, we take the wayposted path on the right (Wp.3 12M). After a short level stretch, the path climbs gently through mixed woodland, crossing a glade glazed with pine needles and going through a gap in a wall onto the **Coll de ne Pollo**, where views along the coast open out. **Sa Costera** is the house below the wood on the distant headland.

The path descends below a high, dry water chute before climbing to pass the first of two gateways with stone hinge brackets. After the second gateway, a clear green field and large reservoir behind **La Fábrica** are visible down to our right. Shortly after a bizarre rock formation that looks like a huge teetering cairn, we come to the signposted path down to 'La Fábrica/Font des Verger' (Wp.4 50M).

Extension / Short Version
Descending 150 metres only to climb right back up again is never a very engaging proposition, but I strongly recommend this extension. Taking the green-arrowed path to the right, we descend steeply, soon coming into view of

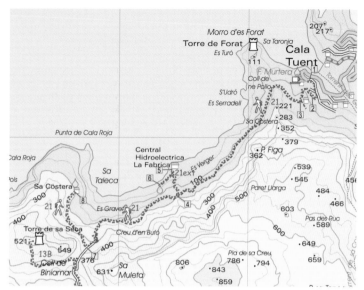

the far end of the reservoir. After crossing a rickety bridge over the reservoir conduit, we bear right, passing a couple of fig trees, and descend to the idyllically situated and beautifully restored generating station (Wp.5 15M from Wp.4). If you want to swim, the steps down to the turbines in front of the main buildings also lead to a tunnel onto what was once a jetty, just to the right of which a rope helps us descend onto the rocks. Turning left at the rickety bridge leads to the spring feeding the conduit (Wp.6). We return by the same route (20M).

To continue to Sa Costera

We follow the main path (W) along long level stretches interrupted by brief and sometimes not so brief climbs. After a clearing on our right, the path widens to a track and we continue climbing for a little over five minutes before taking a wayposted shortcut to the right (Wp.7 80M [not counting the extension]). Thirty metres later, we turn right at another waypost and leave the main trail. Descending along a *carritx* lined path, we bear left at a Y-junction and go through a gap in a wall, after which we follow a terrace to **Sa Costera** (Wp.8 100M), notable for a solar panel supplying a bell that chimes the hours, a mariner's toilet lovingly restored by 'Marti', and (50 metres NW) a tunnel housing a spring. Our return by the same route takes one hour and twenty minutes.

22 THREE PECKS AT THE TORRENT DE PAREIS

The **Torrent de Pareis**, Europe's second largest gorge, is Mallorca's most challenging and popular adventure excursion. However, it can't really be called a 'walk' as some climbing is involved and previous publications have received complaints that it was inappropriate in a walking guide. Bearing this in mind, we developed The Old English Sheepdog Trial, reasoning that anywhere we could go with an Old English Sheepdog, others could follow unencumbered. If you do intend doing the entire descent, enquire first about conditions at the **Serra Tramuntana Information Centre**. Though not essential, a short rope (5-6 metres) is useful for the full descent. Under no circumstances venture into the gorge if there's a risk of rain or the rocks are wet – unless you're one of the daredevils who descend during the winter when it's in full flood; but if you were, you wouldn't be reading a book like this.

(a) BOTTOM UP

This, the easiest of the three routes, is also perhaps the most spectacular, taking us to the mouth of the narrowest part of the gorge. It's not a stroll though and good boots are essential. Take care on the smoother rocks where there's only one way through: so many people have passed, the rocks are not so much polished as burnished. If you want to avoid the crowds (and I mean crowds; just look at the coach-park), arrive early. **Sa Calobra** itself is a splendid little site. What has been done with is somewhat less splendid, but at least it's still public and not smothered in concrete.

| 2 | 1H 40M | 4 km | N ⟋⟍ N | ⟺ | 2 * |

*in **Sa Calobra**

Access: on foot from **Sa Calobra** (accessible by car, boat and bus)

Descending from the **Sa Calobra** car-park, we bear right onto the promenade (0M), at the end of which we go through two dimly lit tunnels onto the pebbly beach at the bottom of the torrent, where we bear right, heading toward the interleaved walls of the gorge.

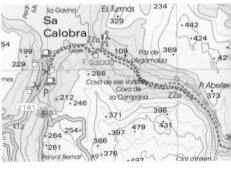

The gorge gradually narrows and, next to an emergency-services sign, we come to a permanent pool (20M). To the left of the pool, we clamber through a natural tunnel formed by an immense rock and the canopy of a fig tree, after which the rocks get bigger, the walls get taller, and we get smaller. Passing a second large fig tree, we cross a slab of rock, after which we start boulder-hopping and squeezing between massive sculpted rocks (there's definitely a touch of the Henry Moores about some of them).

At an immense rock (30M) almost completely blocking the way, the trail appears to bear left, though this in fact ends at a large pool. We bear right to scramble over the rocks. 75 metres later, we bear right again, passing under a looming cavern onto a 50 metre flat stretch leading to the next jumble of boulders (38M). Following the clearly burnished trail, we climb across the middle of the rocks, and approach the narrowest section of the gorge, marked by a distinct menhir-like rock (43M).

The beach at Sa Calobra

The gorge narrows even more, the cliffs climb higher, we continue shrinking. Passing a dripping mossy rock with a small fig tree sprouting from its centre, we squeeze to the left of a long low rock virtually blocking the gorge.

Climbing over (under if you're the dog) a final boulder (150-200 metres after 43M) we come to a 'ladder' of boulders, where you may find a knotted rope (50M). Dogs don't do ladders. We return the same way.

(b) SIDE ON

Hundreds of people stop at the **Nus de Corbata** (Tie Knot) **Mirador** everyday, but none of them seem to realise the car-park is no *mirador* at all. The real *mirador*, to my mind at least, is about a kilometre away at the end of a pathless descent through dense *carritx* and confusing masses of limestone. It's called the **Cingle des Niu des Voltor**, **Vulture's Nest Cliff**, a name that says it all really. Though the walk is short, this is just about the most isolated, little visited spot described in the entire book – take a friend! Also, good boots, long trousers and plenty of water. Rough walking, only for experienced walkers. Beware of rocks hidden by the *carritx*, a perfect man-trap ideal for twisting ankles.

*the Mirador bar is not recommended

Access: by car or bus

From the far end of the **Nus de Corbata** car-park (Wp.1 0M) we follow a faint track that descends towards **Puig Tomir** for 50 metres before petering out above a sheet of dumped bitumen. Ignoring cairns to the left (the start of one Very Mad Mallorcan loop round the **Clot d'Infern**), we maintain direction (ENE) picking our way over the *carritx* and crossing a rocky shelf to find the first of a series of cairns guiding us through our pathless descent.

After crossing a succession of rock sheets, we bear slightly right (ESE) descending into dense vegetation above a gully. Carefully following the cairns (spaced every 5 metres or so), we wind up and down along the southern flank of the gully to an affluent (Wp.2 15M), where we bear left, descending initially in the bed of the affluent, then along its left bank. Towards the bottom,

we re-cross the affluent and descend into the main gully where the walking is slightly easier and the cairns correspondingly fewer.

When the main gully swings left we bear right, passing an outcrop of rock at the head of a long shallow valley (Wp.3 30M). Ignoring cairns that seem to indicate a way along the southern flank of this valley, we descend directly into the valley (NE), aiming for the long roofless building visible on the far side of the gorge (the **Quartel des Carabiners** barracks). For purposes of orientation, the large rocky outcrop just in front of this ruin is the **Serra de ses Farines**. From our perspective, Wp.4 is to the left of this outcrop, Wp.5 to the right. At the bottom of the valley, we descend into a shallow depression, just before which you may see an ancient red waymark. Winding through head high clumps of *carritx*, we cross the depression, on the far side of which we have a choice. Timings assume taking both options.

For a glimpse of the lower stretch of the Pareis and a panorama of uninterrupted rock and sea

We bear left (NNE) and walk alongside the ridge of rock on our left to a pass (Wp.4 55M) at the top of a long slope down to the cliffs. The view is slightly better if you scramble round onto the rocks on your right. Except for the protests of the odd eagle, the silence is absolute. Return to the shallow depression by the same route.

For a more spectacular view from the Vulture's Nest Cliffs

We follow the cairn-marked route (ENE), crossing the lip of the depression and aiming for a distinct eye drilled in the rock, just to the right of which there's a small plateau with a large shady rock (Wp.5 85M) and stunning views towards the **Entreforc** (the junction of the **Gorg Blau** and **Lluc** *torrents*). Take great care here – there is no long slope between you and the cliffs. Return to the **Nus de Corbata** by the same route.

(c) TOP DOWN

A 'peck' is perhaps being a trifle disingenuous for this arduous hike down to the head of the gorge, which is more of a mouthful really. Not recommended on a hot day, but an interesting approach during winter - subject to the usual safety precautions. You might be tempted once at the bottom to continue all the way to **Sa Calobra** rather than slog back up to the top. This temptation should be resisted as the descent between the **Entreforc** and the sea includes all the most difficult passages. If you want to do the full descent, come prepared. Do not improvise. Though laughably easy and little used, the stroll leads to one of the best viewing points overlooking the gorge.

*I haven't used the services, but the **Escorca Restaurant** has a fine terrace and an interesting dining room built into the rock.

Short Version	Stroll
150 metres after Wp.3, as the main path bears sharp left, continue NE toward the olive trees, for a pleasant picnic spot on a grassy *sitja* with great views.	For superb views, carry straight on for 75 metres at Wp.2 onto the long sloping shelf of rock. Note the spectacular rock arch on your left.

Access: by car and bus. Park on the rough ground just west of the **Escorca Restaurant** (km 25 MA-10) rather than in the restaurant car-park.

We start at the western end of the restaurant car-park on a stony path descending between the crash barrier and a multilingual warning notice (Wp.1 0M). Going through a gate almost immediately, we follow a pleasant, shady path alongside terraced pasture, turning left after a second gate before bearing away from the fields (NW). At a metre high cairn (Wp.2 10M), we swing sharp left, following large cairns across the rocks to join a rocky path zigzagging downhill, the **Voltes Llargues** or **Long Bends**, rapidly bringing the gorge into view. Shortly after, we see the **Quartel des Carabiners** barracks and, nestling below **Puig Roig**, the **Coscona** cave houses, the path becomes a little unclear amid the *carritx*, but maintaining our general direction (NNW) we descend toward the top of low cliffs before veering towards the barracks (N) and winding down between rocks beside the partially charred trunk of a fallen tree (Wp.3 25M). We now head in a north-easterly direction before swinging back sharp left to resume our zigzagging descent.

Passing several confused stretches covered in *carritx*, we look out for cairns marking the easier way, sometimes on long zigzags, sometimes on steeper shortcuts (notably at Wp.4 35M). A long north-easterly zig toward the right of **Puig Roig**, during which the entrance to the gorge disappears from view, is followed by an equally long south-westerly zag, before we double back and take a second clear shortcut (Wp.5 40M), soon after which a left hand bend on a broad ledge brings us into view of the remaining, apparently clear zigzags down to the bottom. There is however one tricky spot: after passing under a fig tree, we reach large overhanging rocks. Ignoring the clear way climbing straight ahead, we take a narrow path on the right, descending steeply to the **Torrent de Lluc** (65M) just in front of the **Torrent des Boverons** water chute.

Bearing left, we follow the torrent, picking our way across massive boulders to a faint way through the trees below a cliff (on the left) with an indented watershed. About 50 metres before the gorge narrows, we should, in strict accordance with the Old English Sheepdog Trial, turn back. However, this would be a bit frustrating for bipeds, so I suggest you continue for a further five minutes, descending the easy rocks below the cliff and following the **Torrent de Lluc** to the junction with the **Torrent des Gorg Blau**, the **Entreforc** (90M), where the **Torrent de Pareis** (literally 'Twin Stream') officially begins. From here we may also venture up the **Gorg Blau** torrent to the entrance (no further) of **Sa Fosca**, a complex system of caves and subterranean lakes that can only be explored by fully-equipped, experienced potholers. We return by the same route.

The **Alquería** is the westernmost of the three peaks on our left as we approach the **Sóller** tunnel from **Palma**. It's not a route often walked by tourists, but it is popular with locals and justifiably so. The views are excellent, the middle stretch is pleasantly isolated, and it is nearly all easy walking on dirt tracks that are, for the most part, closed to traffic. There are excellent picnic spots on the peak and after Wp.7.

3 | 3H 5M * | 10 km | 400m 400m | | 0

*40 min from **Bunyola**

Short Versions
(a) A thirty minute climb up the **Alquería** track offers fine views of **Bunyola**, the plain and the **Alquería**'s sister peaks, **Son Poc** and **Son Nassi**. **(b)** In reverse to Wp. 7 (ignore the 'Camino Cortado/Prohibido el paso' signs); easy walking to lovely picnic spots. Wp.9 is the first branch on the left along the **Biniforani Vell** lane.

Extension
If arriving by public transport or staying locally, start from **Bunyola** (see text)

Stroll
Same as extension

Access: by car, bus, train, and on foot from **Bunyola**

Extension
From **Bunyola** church (Wp.1 0M) take the **Carrer de Sant Mateu** (signposted 'Palma') and turn right opposite the **Costa de s'Estacio** street sign. After descending to the main car-park, take the narrow lane past the large ochre-coloured house, **Can Manuel**, for an attractive stroll between gardens and fields to the main road just south of the **S'Alquería d'Avall** farm driveway (Wp.2 20M): km 15.8 of the MA-11, the starting point for motorists.

N.B. Previous reports suggest you cannot park here. In fact, there is room for a few cars and parking seems to be tolerated so long as it doesn't impede access to the driveway.

Taking the **S'Alquería d'Avall** driveway, we bear left just before the house and go through a gate to join a dirt track, which we follow for most of the ascent. Ignoring all branch tracks and paths, we climb steadily through immaculately maintained olive terraces, passing a series of gates. The olives gradually give way to holm-oak, which are in turn interspersed with pine as the views open out across the plain and towards **Bunyola**. Eventually, just after a twin sheepfold, we come to a *coll* where a post topped with a cairn indicates a rough path on the left up to the **Mirador Leandro Ximenis** (Wp.3 80M). Leaving the track, we follow this path past a metal stile and three-sided shelter to the peak (Wp.4 90M), where we have superb views through 360°.

Returning to the dirt track, we bear left for a pleasant stroll passing two gates. After the second gate and directly behind a three-sided hut housing an old cart, we leave the main track and turn right on a minor track (Wp.5 105M) through an olive grove.

After 100 metres the track swings left to cross the olive grove, but we maintain direction (N) for another 400 metres to the end of the olive grove, where an oak forested slope drops steeply away into the **Biniforani** valley. Bearing slightly left, we find a small cairn marking the head of a remarkable little defile, the **Pas de Sa Fesa** (Wp.6 110M).

Pas de Sa Fesa

We descend through the pass, crossing a high-stiled gate midway, to join a steep dirt path zigzagging down through the holm-oak. Towards the bottom, we pass a well-preserved *sitja* and bear left on a gentler slope marked by cairns. We then double back to a large pillar with an iron hinge bracket and descend onto a narrow track above abandoned olive terraces (Wp.7 125M).

Turning left, we wind down through the terraces, crossing a low fence next to green metal gates, after which we join a partially concreted track (Wp.8 135M) leading to a new house. Bearing right, we follow this track through a second set of green gates and, ignoring branches to right and left, continue our descent into the valley, passing a tennis court and a large sunken lemon grove, where we join the tarmac lane (Wp.9 150M) to the **Biniforani Vell** farmhouse. Turning right, we follow this lane for fifteen minutes down to the road, 40 metres north of Wp.2

24 BUNYOLA - PENYALS D'HONOR - BUNYOLA

An attractive tour along mostly shady paths and tracks through the lovely, well-managed forest of **Bunyola**. If you're after solitude, best avoided on a Sunday. If, on the other hand, you care to witness the glorious spectacle of Spanish families enjoying themselves at their gregarious best (just count the generations), Sunday at the **Cas Garriguer Área Recreativa** is a must. To drive or cycle to **Cas Garriguer**, turn left off the MA-2020 just before the playground and follow **Carrer del Garrigó**, signposted 'Sa Comuna'.

* Short Version (a) & (b) each loop 1½ h (c) 1h return . ** in **Bunyola**

Short Versions	Strolls
(a) turn right after Wp.4 to descend via **Comellar d'en Cupí**	**(a)** from Wp.2 continue down the lane back into **Bunyola**
(b) drive to **Cas Garriguer Área Recreativa** then walk back to Wp.6 to join the main walk	**(b)** in almost any direction from the **Área Recreativa**
(c) as per Stroll 'c' but continue to **Cas Garriguer**	**(c)** drive along the MA-2020 past the cemetery. Turn left at the electricity substation, signposted 'Es Cocons', then carry straight on when the main lane bears left (Wp.10). Park on the flat open area (probably with a pile of rubbish in the middle) after **Can Co** and walk up to the troglodytic dwelling.

Access:
on foot from **Bunyola**.

From **Bunyola** church (Wp.1 0M), we take **Carrer Mare de Deú de la Neu** past the post office to cross **Calle de Santa Catalina Tomás** and climb the stairway street, **Carrer de la Lluna**. Turning right at the top, we follow **Carrer d'Orient**, ignoring a first stairway to a private house before turning left onto another stairway street, **Carreró de la Comuna**, signposted 'Sa Comuna/Camí des Grau'. Circling the **Villa Teresa**, we climb to a dirt lane leading towards the mottled bluffs of **El Castellet**. When the lane dips down after 100 metres, we turn left on the **Camí d'es Grau** (Wp.2 10M).

Our path climbs steadily (NE) through the woods to the left of the bluffs, passing the first of the red dots that partially waymark our route. Ignoring all branches, we pass a restored lime-kiln, *sitja* and *aljub* before reaching a Y-junction (Wp.3 25M) where we bear right. After levelling off briefly the **Camí des Grau** continues climbing, zigzagging up to a less well defined stretch winding through the pine. A pleasant meander through the woods brings us to a junction with a broader trail signposted 'Mirador/Camí des Grau' (Wp.4 40M). *Mirador* is a big word for a small clearing on the cliffs with a fallen tree for a bench, but it's only 40 metres to our left, and the views <u>are</u> good. Continuing on the broad trail, we cross a slight rise before joining a dirt track (signed 'Bunyola/Comellar d'en Cupí'), on which we continue climbing through a shallow gully shrouded by a canopy of trees to a major junction of dirt tracks (Wp.5 55M). Turning right, we pass a green fire-fighting reservoir, 50 metres after which we join the main track to **Cas Garriguer** (Wp.6 60M).

Bunyola woods

Ignoring the main track, we immediately bear left on a broad, gated branch track.

The track climbs steadily before levelling out then climbing again. Toward the end of a second long, level stretch, we turn left onto a clear path marked by a cairn and signpost (Wp.7 85M). A steady climb of a little under ten minutes brings us to the white rock of the *penyal*, where there's a small green hut that looks alarmingly like an ice-cream kiosk, but is presumably a weather station (Wp.8 95M). After enjoying the spectacular view, we retrace our steps to Wp.7.

Opposite the path to the *penyal*, another path, almost invisible from the track but marked by a small cairn, descends steadily then steeply before widening and levelling out for a gentle stroll to the last bend in the main track (Wp.9 115M) above the **Cas Garriguer Área Recreativa**. Descending to the turning circle in front of the forest warden's hut (there's also a public refuge - the key is available from **Bunyola** town hall), we maintain direction (SSW) on a broad trail passing picnic tables and barbecues. We follow this trail and the lane it leads into all the way back to **Bunyola**, passing through perhaps the most attractive woodland landscape on the entire island. You don't want to be reading a book while you're wandering through this exquisite wood, so in brief: after thirty minutes the track goes through a green wooden gate and continues between walled olive groves; five minutes later we pass a troglodytic house; just after the **Villa Maria**, we join a lane (Wp.10 180M); ten minutes on this lane brings us to the MA-2020 behind the electricity substation, where we bear right for a fifteen minute walk along the road back to **Bunyola**.

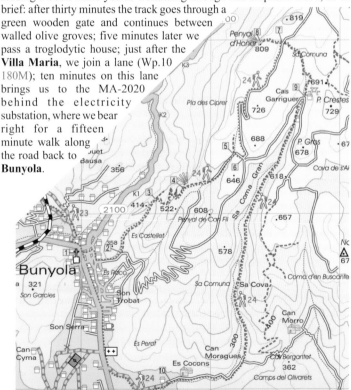

Castell d'Alaró is a <u>very</u> popular walking destination and is best avoided at weekends. Even during the week it's as well to leave early to get there before the guided hiking parties. Most people climb from **Alaró**, but if you have a car, the **Orient** route, on a pleasant, frequently shady path, is far more attractive. Even taking the waymarked shortcuts, the southern approach involves a good three kilometres of wearying tarmac and concrete. The only advantage, apart from public transport, is a more dramatic perspective on the cliffs that made the castle nigh on impregnable (it withstood a siege for two years). The extension, virtually pathless and almost indescribable, is only recommended for those navigating with a GPS 'GoTo' function or the fortunate few possessed of supernatural pathfinding skills.

3	1H 40M *	5 km	350m ** 350m		5 ***

* + 1h for the extension, Short Version 50M
** + 100 metres for the extension
*** The sanctuary can serve 40 and sleep 17, but book if you want to stay or, on weekends, even eat (Tel: 971 182112). The bar's open from 9am-11pm, the kitchen from 12am-4pm & 7-10pm.

Extension see text	**Short Version** Drive to Wp.2 and start from there. Turn west just south of km18 on the MA-2100 then first right and follow the tarmac/concrete lane past **Es Verger** (km 4.5) to **Es Pouet** (km 7) where it ends: note, after the restaurant the track gets even narrower!

Access: by car.

Just after km 11.8 of the MA-2100, 150 metres east of the **Hermitage Hotel**, we take a track climbing into olive groves via a waymarked gate with two signs prohibiting dogs (Wp.1 0M). The broad, chalky white track climbs gently (NE) before narrowing to a well trodden path running along the edge of a terrace. The climb gradually steepens and the path bears right into a shady oak wood. The gradient eases slightly as the oak are interspersed with pine, before a final steady climb brings us onto a track (Wp.2 35M) at the bottom of the gently shelving clearing of **Es Pouet**.

At the top of the clearing, we bear left at the 'Alaró/Santuari y Postat Hostatgeria del Castell d'Alaró' signpost onto long, shallow steps leading to a partially cobbled trail. At the junction with the old path from **Alaró** (Wp.3 50M), we bear left and follow the remaining steps up to the castle gates.

After exploring (cautiously!) the battlements along the west of the ridge, we follow the stone trail (E) up to the sanctuary (Wp.4 60M). Taking the partially ramped steps to the right of the chapel and climbing to the aerial, we can see (E) **Alaró**'s twin peak, **s'Alcaldena**.

Extension

The path to the **Cova de San Antoni** is so obscure it barely exists, but even those wholly lacking a sense of direction can enjoy wandering round the woods to the east, visiting the lime-kilns and *aljibes*. For the more adventurous, cairns mark the way down to the cave, which can be explored, but only with the utmost care and NOT when it's wet.

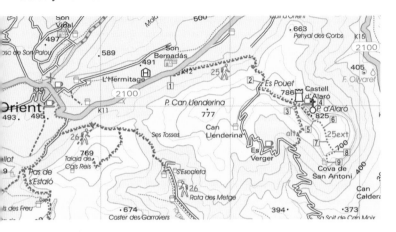

The onward 'path' begins at the end of the sanctuary terrace, beyond the rough wooden gate where the donkeys are corralled.

GPS users turn to their 'GoTo' function here, but be careful: there's no such thing as a straight line through these woods and you still need to follow the cairns carefully. After Wp.6, if you haven't seen a cairn in the preceding 30 metres, go back to the last cairn and look again. The route takes about twenty-five minutes each way. Given the inevitable pausing, peering and backtracking required to find the cairns, partial times are redundant, but the following waypoints were taken at roughly five minute intervals.

At first the path is reasonably clear, passing an outdoor privy and winding between rocks (ESE) to cross two linked clearings (Wp.5). Continuing through the woods (SE), look for a third clearing (Wp.6) a few metres to the right of the main path, where we bear right to pass a lime-kiln. We now follow the cairns in a more southerly direction, passing Wp.7 (solely a GPS bearing, indistinguishable from the surrounding woodland) and steadily descending until, off to our right, we can see a partially ruined watchtower perched on the cliffs (Wp.8). Bearing right (SW), we follow a reasonably clear path down to the tower (Wp.9). The entrance to the cave is a small hole, 15 metres before the tower. We return via the same route. The descent from the sanctuary to the starting point takes about forty minutes.

26 ORIENT: PASTURE, PASSES AND A PEAK

Our previous walk in **Orient** involved an obscure scramble up the **Torrent des Bous**. However, I know of at least one couple who simply never found their way up (don't worry, they did get back all right), and since there doesn't seem to be a lot of point publishing itineraries so devious nobody else can follow them, we decided a new walk was needed. Setting off from the pleasant pastoral valley of **Orient**, we climb to a wonderful natural mirador on the **Talaia de Cals Reis**, then descend toward **Alaró** via the extraordinary **Pas de s'Escaleta**, after which a gruelling climb brings us back onto the wooded heights to return via the only marginally less impressive **Pas de s'Estaló** . Working from maps alone (the walk was made up 'on the hoof'), it took us dark ages to find the way between Wps. 16&18, but if you follow the directions, you shouldn't have any difficulty.

Short Version: to the **Talaia de Cals Reis** *mirador*, returning via the same route.

Access: on foot from **Orient**. There is a taxibus service to **Orient** from **Bunyola** (which can be reached by train and bus) bookable a day in advance on 971615219 or 609690553. If arriving by the taxibus, bear in mind, 3h20 is a 'pure' time. You should allow at least five hours for the full walk.

From the busstop/parking area immediately south of **Orient** (Wp.1 0M), we walk up the road for 275 metres toward the **Hermitage Hotel** and **Alaró** , then turn right in front of a large reservoir (Wp.2 4M) to go through a red gate into an orchard, where we bear left on a dirt track climbing (SW) to the oak forested slopes on the southern flank of the valley. After going through a gate into the woods, we turn left (Wp.3 9M) and follow a charcoal burners' trail climbing along the edge of the woods.

Ignoring a minor branch on the right (Wp.4 17M), we go through a gap in a wall, after which the trail levels off, following a terrace in an easterly direction before climbing briefly to the crest of a slight rise, where cairns on our right indicate the linear ascent of the **Talaia de Cals Reis** (Wp.5 22M).

At first, the **Talaia** branch is faint, but the way soon becomes a broad, rough trail that in turn dwindles to a narrow path (Wp.6 31M), 40 metres along which we enter a denser stand of oak. A steep climb brings us to a wall (Wp.7 39M), where we turn right and head north for 75 metres to a rocky platform that serves as a natural *mirador*, with superb views over the

Orient from the mirador

Orient valley and a large stretch of the **Tramuntana** (Wp.8 41M). There is an off-path route continuing to the west from here marked with the very occasional cairn, but it is indiscernible and indescribable (we got to within 300 metres of Wp.20 before giving it up as a bad job), so I recommend returning to Wp.5 (54M) by the same route.

Heading east on the main path, we fork

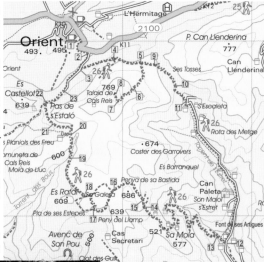

Pas de s'Escaleta

right at a Y-junction 150metres after the **Talaia** turnoff (Wp.9) and follow a narrow path descending through lovely, fairytale woodland to the **Pas de s'Escaleta** (Wp.10 64M), a runoff channel carved into a rocky declivity, where a small wall has been built, inset with steps to aid the descent

Beyond the pas a good path zigzags down to join a concrete track, where we turn right (Wp.11 73M). We follow this track for the best part of two kilometres, initially descending steeply through a series of zigzags, then on an easier gradient shadowing the **Torrent de s'Estret**, enjoying the easy walking and picturesque scenery very picturesque, look out for the Indian guru with a Great Dane!

Eventually, we reach the covered and locked **Font de ses Artigues** and the cluster of houses of the same name. Immediately after the font, we turn right, stepping over a low, broken wall beside a locked gate (Wp.12 103M) then bearing left 75 metres later on a dirt track (Wp.13) that climbs very steeply across abandoned terraces. This is the toughest stretch of the walk, so take your time and stop occasionally to enjoy the view over the **Estret** valley behind you, because the track of itself isn't terribly beguiling. The track levels off briefly toward the top, but the punishing climb soon resumes, passing a succession of cabins and curving round below the streaked cliffs of the **Mola de sa Bastida** to approach the spinelike outcrop of **Sa Galera**.

Eventually, after what seems like forever, we pass two forks off to the right within 100 metres of each other (Wp.14 144M & Wp.15) and, 200 metres later, go through a gate (or by pass it to the right if it's locked), whereupon we relax, as the really hard work is done, though some care is required for pathfinding in the next fifteen minutes. Ignoring a branch off to the right 225 metres after the gate (Wp.16 153M), we stay on the main track till it reaches the entrance of the **Es Rafal** ruin (Wp.17 157M). Bearing right, we follow the track to the north for 150metres, then west for 75metres to go through a gap in a wall directly behind the ruin. Turning right on the far side of the wall (Wp.18), we follow a faint way running alongside the wall, at the end of which a cairn confirms that we are on trail.

The end of the walk is pure pleasure as we stroll along a narrow path well-marked with cairns, weaving our way through dense woodland and passing the head of the **Torrent des Bous**, where our old itinerary emerged, or not according to your experience (a couple of cairns suggest some people still make it) (Wp.19 169M). The path then climbs across exposed rock and goes through a gap in a wall (Wp.20 174M), after which a steady descent takes us past a miniature reservoir.

Pas de s'Estalo

Following a contour, we cross a sheet of exposed rock (Wp.21 179M), 250metres after which we join the broad trail crossing the **Pas de s'Estaló** (Wp.22 183M). Turning right then left 350 metres later (Wp.23), we rejoin our outward route at Wp.3.

Puig de Massanella, Mallorca's highest accessible summit (**Puig Major**, the highest, being a military installation), is conventionally climbed via a paying route through the **Comafreda** estate. In the original edition of this book, seized by a somewhat harumphing mood of 'Damned-if-I'll-pay-to-go-walking', I opted for an off-path scramble circumventing the gatekeeper's lodge via the **Cometa Negra** torrent. I'm a little less puritanical about such things than I used to be and have to admit that asking people to pay a small fee (4 euros) to cross private property certainly beats pocketing the government stipend guaranteeing public access then purchasing a padlock and a *Prohibido el Paso* sign with the proceeds, which is not unknown elsewhere. In this new version of the itinerary, I've re-walked a variant of the off-path ascent (featuring more razor sharp limestone and less clambering over dead trees), and included the paying route on the return, allowing us to finish the walk with an easy descent on the **Cami Vell** featured as an ascent in Walk 30. If you have any doubts about the offpath bit after reading the description, don't attempt it, it really is very tough, and just stick with the paying route that begins beside the bridge below **Coll de sa Batalla**, following Wps. 9-21 in reverse. If you do the off-path ascent, tell someone where you're going: I can almost guarantee you won't see anybody up here and there's plenty of scope for accidents.

N.B. GPS reception is patchy in the torrent, not geographically but temporally some days it's clear, others not!

We start from the tunnel under the road in the **Sa Coveta Área Recreativa** at km10 of the MA2130 (Wp.1 0M), on the far side of which a stile leads onto a dirt track, where there's a Camina per Mallorca mapboard and a signpost for the 'GR222 Lluc 1h30'. After passing a memorial to Isabel Morel Morro (Wp.2 8M), we climb steadily to a junction where the main track doubles back to the right (Wp.3 13M), at which point we leave the GR and carry straight on along a minor track that rapidly deteriorates to a rough trail.

At the top of an S-bend (Wp.4 17M), a large cairn indicates where we leave the trail and climb to the right, off path, following old red waymarks and, above all, regular cairns if you haven't seen a cairn in twenty metres, turn back until you find one.

Massanella seen from Canaleta Walk 19

Climbing steadily through the woods (NW), we initially follow the intermittent remains of charcoal-burners' trails, but these soon disappear and, after traversing several sheets of rock, we reach an affluent of the main torrent where there's a large red dot (Wp.5 26M). This is where the going gets tough, as we scramble up the increasingly vicious rocks to our left. Again, no cairn, no go!

Pathfinding is a real problem here, so though the climb across the limestone is relatively brief, you need to take your time, favouring the left hand side of the rocks but regularly veering right to break the gradient. It'll probably take you about ten minutes to cover the 100 metres on the rock, but once past it, the cairns guide us through scruffy, unkempt wood for a slightly easier climb to cross a tiny patch of wall built about the broad bole of a twin-trunked pine (Wp.6 45M) at the **Pas de n'Arbona**.

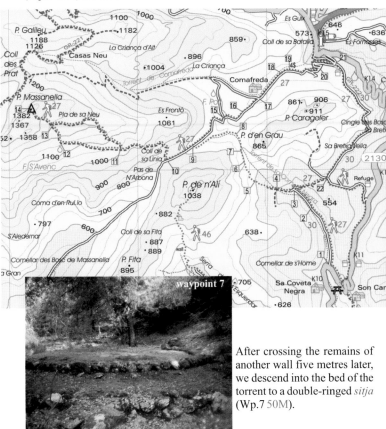

After crossing the remains of another wall five metres later, we descend into the bed of the torrent to a double-ringed *sitja* (Wp.7 50M).

In many ways, this is the wildest part of the walk, but progress is considerably easier and pathfinding is not really a problem as we now simply have to stay in the bed of the torrent, picking out the easiest route while keeping an eye out for the cairns and occasional waymarks.

Crossing countless *sitjes*, we follow the torrent in a northerly direction and stay with it when it veers left (Wp.8 55M). After a little over another 500 metres, the cairn marked route climbs to the right to join the main track between the **Comafreda** and **Massanella** estates (Wp.9 68M).

Bearing left, we climb to the **Coll de sa Linia** (Wp.10 74M), identifiable by two large, stone marker posts. Turning right, we take a clear path between the marker posts that climbs through the woods to a triangular concrete marker post (Wp.11 99M) indicating 'Font y Puig' on the left and 'Puig y Font' on the right.

The latter is the easier way to the top, but if you want to do both routes, I suggest passing by the **S'Avenc** spring first as a steep climb is less risky than a steep descent. Beware, though: the spring route traverses rough, pathless terrain, and there's a maze of divergent, cairn marked ways, most of which go nowhere! It is essential to follow the lower route marked with cairns AND red waymarks. If you find the cairns are getting increasingly infrequent and the waymarks have disappeared, you're on a false trail. Go back till you find regular cairns and waymarks. Particular care must be taken in the first 200 metres after the marker stone. ALWAYS look for the lower cairns, even if the cairns climbing to the right seem to mark a clearer way.

Staying more or less on the level and only climbing slightly, never steeply, we follow the cairns and waymarks (W) until we pass a large bushy oak, beyond which the real climb begins, initially on rubble, but soon passing a sloping rock shelf with five marker steps cemented onto it. A steady climb across the rocks, passing waymarks, cairns and the occasional cemented marker-step brings us abreast of the 'Font de s'Avenc' (Wp.12 114M), where steps descend to the spring and a damp shelter with rough stone benches and a table.

Just after the spring, cairns mark the way up the jagged limestone crowning the mountain. A steep climb gradually brings us into view of the trig point on the peak. After passing another triangular marker stone (Wp.13 129M), the gradient eases briefly and, 100 metres later, we join the 'easy' path from the **Pla de sa Neu** or Snow Plain, where we bear left for the final slog up to the summit (Wp.14 149M).

After taking in the views and staying well back from the alarming drops on the northern side of the summit, we retrace our way back to the 'easy' route across the **Pla de sa Neu** (E), at the end of which the trail bears right (SSE) to go through a natural gateway onto a good path zigzagging down to Wp.10 (209M).

From Wp.9 (214M), we can either return the same way, or (recommended) opt for the far easier paying route and the **Cami Vell**. The main **Comafreda** track descends in an easterly direction, passing a large ruin, 150 metres after which, cairns and waymarks indicate a path on our right (Wp.15 223M). The path soon goes through a gap in a wall (Wp.16 227M), after which it broadens to a rough trail leading to the main track in front of the **Comafreda** farmhouse (Wp.17 232M). A couple of hundred metres after passing a rough fork off to the right (Wp.18 233M), we reach the gatekeeper and fuss about with our purses (Wp.19) then continue on our way the lighter by 4 euros.

Ignoring a first track off to the right (Wp.20), we descend to a second junction, where two tracks branch off to the right (Wp.21 245M), the lower of which is the wayposted **Camí Vell**. We now simply follow this fabulous old trail back to the start, bearing right at a signposted junction at the foot of a long straight cobbled section (Wp.22 266M) and crossing a small coll to rejoin our outward route at Wp.3 (274M).

See the notes on GPS use and waypoints on pages 18-19.

9.Sóller - Port de Sóller - Sóller

Wp	N	E
1	39 46.2995	2 43.0245
2	39 46.3715	2 42.9615
3	39 46.4935	2 42.6715
4	39 46.5975	2 42.5185
5	39 46.8815	2 42.4175
6	39 46.9675	2 42.3805
7	39 47.1835	2 42.4225
8	39 47.2675	2 42. 4095
9	39 47.3745	2 42.3875
10	39 47.4315	2 42.3595
11	39 47.8965	2 42.5775
12	39 47.9205	2 42.0745
13	39 47.6885	2 42.2125
Alt1	39 47.1085	2 42.4665
Alt2	39 46.8615	2 42.6735

10.Three Villages + One Thundering Great Climb

Wp	N	E
1	39 46.2864	2 43.0344
2	39 46.6200	2 43.5648
3	39 47.0292	2 44.4282
4	39 47.5098	2 44.3844
5	39 47.5992	2 44.2326
6	39 47.4306	2 43.5030
7	39 47.1432	2 43.9302
8	39 46.9692	2 44.0694

11.The Ultimate Picnic Walk - Torre Picada & Sa Illeta

Wp	N	E
1	39 47.8056	2 41.8002
2	39 48.1116	2 42.1242
3	39 48.3120	2 41.1272
4	39 48.3858	2 41.8362
5	39 48.5718	2 42.4824
6	39 48.8010	2 42.7818
7	39 49.1166	2 43.2984
8	39 48.9180	2 42.8022

12.Capelleta & Campo

Wp	N	E
1	39 46.4172	2 43.2162
2	39 46.6962	2 43.3188
3	39 46.8450	2 43.3428
4	39 47.0676	2 43.3938
5	39 47.3580	2 43.2096
6	39 47.0628	2 42.9804

13a.Mirador de ses Barques

Wp	N	E
1	39 47.6226	2 42.8856
2	39 47.3592	2 43.2138
3	39 47.5518	2 43.4538
4	39 47.8026	2 43.5978
5	39 47.4552	2 43.4934
6	39 47.2542	2 43.4160
7	39 47.1456	2 43.4274

13b.Torre de na Seca

Wp	N	E
1	39 47.4555	2 43.5015
2	39 47.4875	2 43.5755
3	39 47.8045	2 43.5985
4	39 47.2545	2 43.8215
5	39 48.3925	2 43.9274
6	39 48.5775	2 44.3805
7	39 48.8075	2 44.4755
8	39 48.9315	2 44.5935
9	39 49.1785	2 44.6915
10	39 49.2975	2 44.6515
11	39 49.2685	2 44.3025
12	39 49.4205	2 44.2795

14. L'Ofre

Wp	N	E
1	39 47.2365	2 47.8155
2	39 46.6895	2 46.7115
3	39 46.1865	2 46.0945
4	39 45.9665	2 45.7895
5	39 46.0135	2 46.3615
6	39 45.9765	2 46.3735
7	39 45.8035	2 46.0705
8	39 45.6385	2 46.0675
9	39 45.5745	2 46.0435
E1	39 45.6432	2 45.5892
E2	39 45.5976	2 45.3960
E3	39 46.1982	2 44.0784

Biniaraix to Sóller

Wp	N	E
BS1	39 46.2785	2 44.1705
BS2	39 46.2825	2 44.0995
BS3	39 46.4245	2 43.8515
BS4	39 46.3485	2 43.1825
BS5	39 46.2955	2 43.0365

15. Rateta

Wp	N	E
1	39 47.2365	2 47.8165
2	39 46.8535	2 47.5365
3	39 46.6025	2 47.8315
4	39 46.4895	2 47.8235
5	39 46.3825	2 47.7785
6	39 46.4255	2 47.6835

Wp	N	E
7	39 46.3585	2 47.4895
8	39 46.3225	2 47.3455
9	39 46.3435	2 47.1805
10	39 46.2865	2 47.1085
11	39 46.4355	2 47.0585
12	39 46.4095	2 46.9285
13	39 46.2525	2 46.7535
14	39 46.1334	2 46.5570
15	39 45.9504	2 46.3554
16	39 46.2258	2 46.3818
17	39 46.2390	2 46.1508
18	39 46.5565	2 46.6145

16. Tossals Verds Circuit

Wp	N	E
1	39 47.2272	2 47.9742
2	39 46.8486	2 47.5326
3	39 46.5246	2 48.1164
4	39 46.0170	2 48.6132
5	39 45.8688	2 48.8160
6	39 46.0992	2 49.1322
7	39 46.6182	2 49.8342
8	39 47.1678	2 49.8870
9	39 47.2716	2 49.7154
10	39 47.3118	2 49.5174
11	39 47.5242	2 49.4292

17. Twin Peaks & One Mad Mallorcan Loop

Wp	N	E
1	39 47.2458	2 47.9652
2	39 47.5284	2 49.4256
3	39 47.3136	2 49.5258
4	39 47.2494	2 49.3434
5	39 47.2086	2 49.1772
6	39 47.3598	2 49.1160
7	39 47.0046	2 49.0710
8	39 47.0526	2 49.2240
9	39 47.1516	2 48.8874
10	39 47.2248	2 48.6912
11	39 47.0850	2 48.4782
12	39 47.0394	2 48.3828
13	39 47.0382	2 48.3336
14	39 47.0286	2 48.1782
15	39 47.0610	2 48.0612

18. The Alfábia Ridge

Wp	N	E
1	39 45.6942	2 43.1616
2	39 45.4770	2 43.1070
3	39 45.3774	2 43.1142
4	39 45.2250	2 42.9972
5	39 45.0894	2 42.9816
6	39 44.8674	2 42.9360

	N	E
7	39 44.8212	2 42.9576
8	39 44.5710	2 42.9798
9	39 44.3940	2 43.0260
10	39 44.2398	2 43.2216
11	39 44.3976	2 43.6080
12	39 44.6016	2 43.9470
13	39 44.6562	2 44.1006
14	39 44.7870	2 44.3502
15	39 45.0096	2 44.4732
16	39 45.1272	2 44.6634
17	39 45.4944	2 44.8434
18	39 45.5550	2 45.3576

19 Canaleta

Wp	N	E
1	39 47.2485	2 47.9705
2	39 47.5285	2 49.4225
3	39 47.3135	2 49.5235
4	39 47.2515	2 49.7035
5	39 47.2795	2 49.7185
6	39 47.3745	2 49.8435
7	39 47.1815	2 49.8615
8	39 46.8915	2 50.1595
9	39 46.8205	2 50.3215
10	39 46.9215	2 50.5785
11	39 47.0155	2 50.9335
12	39 47.1415	2 49.8865

20. La Mola de Tuent

Wp	N	E
1	39 50.5500	2 47.2248
2	39 50.7672	2 47.2254
3	39 50.7930	2 47.1660
4	39 50.8962	2 47.0160

21. Cala Tuent - Sa Costera - Cala Tuent

Wp	N	E
1	39 50.3526	2 46.4940
2	39 50.2536	2 46.4742
3	39 50.2074	2 46.3854
4	39 49.6620	2 45.4578
5	39 49.7976	2 45.3906
6	39 49.7130	2 45.3228
7	39 49.3722	2 44.7528
8	39 49.6914	2 44.6502

22. Torrent de Pareis

(b)

Wp	N	E
1	39 49.9230	2 48.9912
2	39 49.9446	2 49.2402
3	39 50.0370	2 49.3344
4	39 50.1900	2 49.4730
5	39 50.1840	2 49.6920

(c)

Wp	N	E
1	39 49.5726	2 50.8230
2	39 49.7778	2 50.6136
3	39 49.8750	2 50.4846
4	39 49.9434	2 50.5200
5	39 50.0184	2 50.4654

23. Bunyola - Alquería - Bunyola

Wp	N	E
1	39 41.7636	2 41.9898
2	39 42.3696	2 41.3490
3	39 41.9808	2 40.4496
4	39 41.8374	2 40.4448
5	39 42.2358	2 40.3212
6	39 42.4482	2 40.3578
7	39 42.5688	2 40.4082
8	39 42.7260	2 40.4274
9	39 42.8958	2 40.7568

24. Bunyola - Penyal d'Honor - Bunyola

Wp	N	E
1	39 41.7912	2 41.9700
2	39 41.7774	2 42.2958
3	39 42.0702	2 42.5316
4	39 42.1470	2 42.7626
5	39 42.3624	2 43.1874
6	39 42.3222	2 43.2420
7	39 42.9732	2 43.5276
8	39 42.9834	2 43.3686
9	39 42.6576	2 43.7064
10	39 41.0471	2 42.7222

25. Castell d'Alaró & Cova de Sant Antoni

Wp	N	E
1	39 44.1948	2 46.5168
2	39 44.1300	2 47.2104
3	39 43.9620	2 47.5320
4	39 43.9500	2 47.5908
5	39 43.9104	2 47.6508
6	39 43.8816	2 47.7294
7	39 43.8060	2 47.7468
8	39 43.7478	2 47.7942
9	39 43.6740	2 47.7450

26. Orient

Wp	N	E
1	39 44.0195	2 45.6835
2	39 43.9555	2 45.7585
3	39 43.8285	2 45.6595
4	39 43.8905	2 45.9345
5	39 43.8875	2 46.1425

	N	E
6	39 43.7455	2 46.0845
7	39 43.6785	2 45.9625
8	39 43.7185	2 45.9455
9	39 43.8725	2 46.2415
10	39 43.7575	2 46.3935
11	39 43.6685	2 46.4825
12	39 42.8545	2 46.7835
13	39 42.8775	2 46.7375
14	39 43.0585	2 46.1695
15	39 43.0965	2 46.1535
16	39 43.1485	2 45.9305
17	39 43.0515	2 45.7565
18	39 43.1065	2 45.6985
19	39 43.3365	2 45.5835
20	39 43.4685	2 45.5985
21	39 43.5196	2 45.4614
22	39 43.6364	2 45.3986
23	30 43.7593	2 45.5833

27. Puig Massanella

Wp	N	E
1	39 47.4584	2 53.4566
2	39 47.7833	2 53.3294
3	39 47.8934	2 53.2246
4	39 47.8745	2 53.0906
5	39 47.9783	2 52.9695
6	39 48.0386	2 52.8474
7	39 48.1158	2 52.8276
8	39 48.2034	2 52.7595
9	39 48.1345	2 52.4334
10	39 48.0458	2 52.2624
11	39 48.1104	2 51.8850
12	39 48.1410	2 51.4284
13	39 48.2310	2 51.3546
14	39 48.3618	2 51.1788
15	39 48.2805	2 52.6905
16	39 48.3045	2 52.8105
17	39 48.4105	2 52.9566
18	39 48.5305	2 53.0844
19	39 48.5775	2 53.1834
20	39 48.5866	2 53.4195
21	39 48.6085	2 53.5456
22	39 47.9555	2 53.4914

A place of Pilgrimage, Tormented Trees & Tethered Islands

The monastery at **Lluc** is in many ways the spiritual home of Mallorca. When the church was still the most potent trans-national institution in Europe, **Lluc** was the objective of traditional pilgrimages, many of which continue to this day, though socializing rather than salvation appears to be the prime motive now, even among avowedly Christian groups; with the advent of mass tourism, restaurants and an immense, charmless car-park were installed to accommodate package pilgrims for whom the church's function was principally decorative, more a focus for the camera lens. Nowadays the **Tramuntana Information Centre** at the monastery gates is a magnet for modern nature pilgrims, come to worship at the altar of landscape, flora and fauna, and practice their devotions on some of the island's finest footpaths.

After **Lluc**, the road tempts us into a long, free-wheeling descent to **Pollença**, but it's worth pulling over at least twice en route to enjoy the remarkable landscape. First stop is the area between the **Binifaldó** and **Mossa** estates, a shadowy jigsaw of chaotic limestone pavement and fluted calcareous rock speckled with holm oak, olive and pine, and carpeted with great swathes of asphodels and banks of moss. It's a delightful place for a stroll through the woods, either from the access road to the **Binifaldó** bottling plant or one of the excellent *áreas recreativa* on the main road, which also happen to be among the few places on the island where camping is allowed.

Further down the MA-10, another tremendously privileged spot lies between the road and the northern coast, encompassed by the **Mortitx**, **Havanor** and **Rafal d'Ariant** estates. Everywhere you go in Mallorca, you'll be amazed by ancient olive trees twisted into incredibly contorted shapes, some so monolithic and gnarled by repeated pollarding, they resemble monstrous lumps of solid rock endeavouring, with invincible optimism, to pass themselves off as fruitful trees by the feeble ruse of decking themselves out with a few flimsy twigs and sprays of pale green leaves. George Sand compared these trees to fairytale monsters, while Rusiñol got so excited he spoke of "such hysterical convulsions they can hardly be called trees; they are more like epileptics"! Such images probably tell us more about the authors than the trees, but they serve to convey a sense of the thousands of small, arboreal epiphanies to be experienced on the island, and **Mortitx** is one the best places to enjoy them.

Eventually, the broad green valley behind **Pollença** opens out and we head down to the eastern plain. The old towns of **Pollença** and **Alcúdia** are worth visiting while their respective ports serve their purpose as tourist towns with a full range of facilities, but the real stars at this end of the island are the two peninsulas tipped by the **Caps de Formentor** and **Pinar**. The necks of these peninsulas are in the first case so narrow and in the second so shallow they look like they've been haphazardly moored to the main island and could as easily be untethered and set adrift. This impression of being all at sea is compounded as you drive onto **Formentor**, which appears to be composed of a series of discrete sails, like a regatta of rock. Even if you haven't got a car, hire a bike or taxi to get up to the **Coll de la Creuta** *mirador* for a glimpse of this magnificent spectacle: you won't regret it.

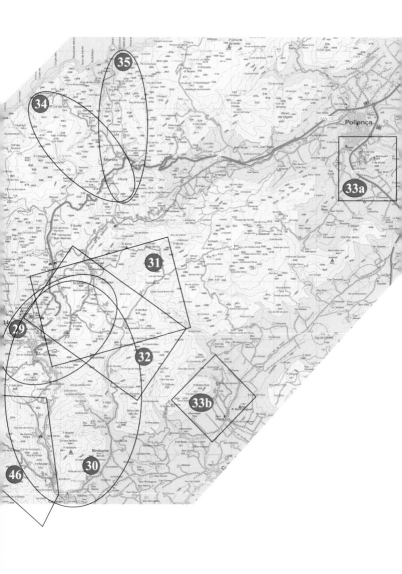

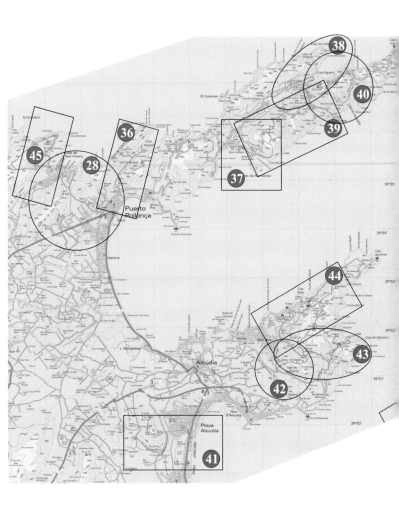

This very popular walk crosses the **Siller Pass** between **Port de Pollença** and **Cala St. Vicenç** (actually four tiny creeks or *calas* clustered together in a large bay). It's very easy, you can do the main walk in sandals or tennis shoes, and ideal for a family stroll - I've even seen a young mother coming from **Cala St. Vicenç** with a pushchair! The extension onto **Serra de la Punta**, by contrast, is rough walking, requiring good footwear and a taste for hopping about on rocky terrain with nothing but cairns and mountain goats for company.

* Extension 4 - **Serra de la Punta**, see text.
** 3h15 including the extension *** + 225 metres for the extension

Access: on foot from **Port de Pollença** or **Cala St. Vicenç**.

From the seafront in **Port de Pollença**, we take the **Pollença** road (**Carrer de Joan XXIII**) and turn right at **Bar Juanito**, 20 metres before the ELF/Cepsa petrol station, on **Carrer de Cala St. Vicenç** (Wp.1 0M). Crossing the new bypass, we take **Carrer de les Roses** to the left of the beige house with blue shutters. Ignoring four branches on the right, we follow **Carrer de les Roses** into open countryside to head for **Elcano** boatyard.

At the quadruple fork between the boatyard and the 'L'Hort de Siller', we carry straight on along a well-stabilized track. When the track swings left into a private house, we continue on a rougher dirt track. When this track also swings left (Wp.2 15M), we bear right on a broad walking trail. The trail climbs gently at first, then more steeply as it narrows to a path, which runs into a dirt track, 150 metres from a water-hut on the **Coll de Siller** (Wp.3 25M). Seventy five metres after the *coll* we pass a narrow cairn-marked way on our left. This is the extension. 50 metres after that, just before the track goes under the telephone cable, we take a clearer path to the left, winding across a *carritx* covered slope toward **Cala St. Vicenç**. Passing numerous cairns and a Y-junction (the two branches soon rejoin), we cross a shallow gully and go through a small pine wood, where the path broadens to a trail descending alongside a fence to a concrete lane (Wp.4 35M) which we follow down to a T-junction.

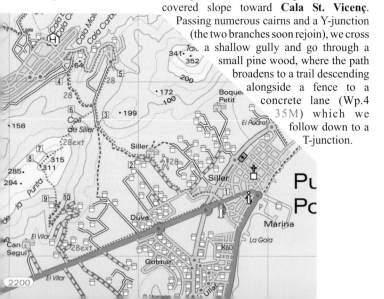

We bear right to descend past **Hostal Los Pinos** to a second T-junction.

Bearing right again, we can either take
the stairway directly into **Cala St.
Vicenç** (45M) for refreshment (on the
road running along the spine between
Cala Clara and **Cala Molins** if the
tourist spots nearer the beach are
closed) and to visit the bronze age
burial mound (further up the same
road), or we can continue along the
partially asphalted road toward the sea
to take the 'pushchair' route back
toward **Coll de Siller**.

Cala Carbó

To return to Coll de Siller. We bear right along the seafront and follow the
road as it winds up the gully (which we crossed earlier) behind **Cala Carbó**.
The road swings left, climbs to a modernist villa and briefly levels out.
Ignoring a branch to our left, we climb again and bear right into a large
roundabout, from which we take the second branch on the left (Wp.5 55M)
back to **Coll de Siller** (65M).

Extension. Waypoint times are counted from the **Coll de Siller** track. Though
pathless, the way is well marked with cairns and, if you look up toward the
unnamed 315 metre summit (a wonderful wild little spot with excellent
views), the climb behind the easternmost outcrop of rock and then directly up
onto the summit is fairly obvious.

Leaving the track at the second-maybe-first pine (see above), we cross a low
wall and follow a line of fencing posts (W). 30 metres from the western end of
the fencing posts, we find a second cairn (Wp.6 3M), where we bear slightly
left and head for the ridge. During the climb you'll be too busy watching
where you put your feet and looking for the next cairn to be reading
descriptions, in any case largely superfluous on such featureless terrain, but in
brief: picking our way from cairn to cairn and passing occasional dull red
waymarks, we climb steadily then steeply across increasingly rough ground
(WSW) before zigzagging up to scramble directly over the rocks to the large
pile of stones marking the top (Wp.7 45M).

Following the ridge (W) for 150 metres, we bear sharp left on the second little
top at a tall thin cairn next to a red waymark (Wp.8 50M) and head for the large
boat park by the main road. Ignoring the main cairn-marked way along the
ridge, we maintain a southerly direction to pass a red waymark from where we
can see another cairn below us in a direct line with the marina. Bearing
slightly right after this cairn, we aim for the long spur that ends in two flat-
roofed concrete buildings backed by what appears to be a round reservoir (in
fact a dry-stone corral). Maintaining direction (S) and always heading for the
spur, we hop from rock to rock and pick our way through the *carritx*,
descending steadily to another large waymarked rock (Wp.9 80M) at the top
of the spur, where we join a badly overgrown broad track, zigzagging down it
to the top of **El Vilar** *urbanización* (Wp.10 95M). After descending through
the *urbanización* to the MA-2200 (105M), we turn left for a rather dreary
trudge on the main road back to **Port de Pollença** (130M).

29 LLUC - BINIFALDÓ - LLUC

Though it features no outstanding summits or spectacularly wild corners, this is a very easy and very pleasant introduction to the karst and woodlands around **Lluc**, visiting the famous **Camel Rock** and crossing an astonishing rock garden.

| 2 | (3H) * | 11.5 km | ∧∨ | 200m 200m | ↻ | 3 ** |

* Short Version 50M (estimated) ** in **Lluc**

| **Stroll: to the Camel Rock** and back. |

Access: by car or bus

From the **Serra Tramuntana Information Centre** (Wp.1 0M), we follow the monastery access road toward the MA-10 then turn left after 150-metres (immediately after the GR turns right) onto a tarmac drive, and then right to go through a stone gateway marked with a red dot. After crossing the football pitch and a wooden bridge at its far left corner, we take the waymarked steps climbing steadily through a chaos of delicately fluted rock.

'Camel Rock'

Fifty metres after the steps give way to a dirt path, there's a *sitja* on our left flanked by a stone bench and a log rubbish bin, 5 metres before which, a signpost to the right indicates the path to 'Es Camell', three minutes away on a good path (Wp.2 10M) along with Spanish graffiti claiming it's an elephant, not a camel, and that you've got to be drunk to see it!

Continuing on the main path (N), we climb to a level junction of dirt trails, where we turn left for 'Es Pixarells'. After crossing a gentle rise, we pass two benches with fine views of the **Puigs Roig** and **Caragoler**, then zigzag into a shallow depression, passing a series of *sitjes* and rocks riddled by erosion. Bearing right then left out of the depression, we climb to the **Es Pixarells Área Recreativa**, where we take the partially concreted track up towards the MA-10.Below the **Área Recreativa** noticeboard and in front of the water point, we take a narrow path through the woods behind the parking bays (Wp.3 40M).

After passing a *sitja* and crossing a small outcrop of rock, we descend on cobbled steps towards a flat, rock fringed glade, formerly a designated camping area, as attested by the stubby posts marking tent placements (camping is forbidden here now). At the bottom of the steps, we turn right on a rough way climbing over rocks to a path leading into a labyrinth of rocks alongside the MA-10. After passing an old red waymarking arrow, we bear left at a waypost and almost immediately find another waypost and a *sitja*. Maintaining direction, we cross two large outcrops of rock, hopefully with cairns on them, to a third tall waypost, where we bear left again on a reasonably clear stretch leading to an apparent dead-end in a small glade. Just to the right of this glade there's an electricity pylon and two cairns marking a way across the rocks to the right of the pylon, after which a clear path back to the road emerges at a gateway directly in front of the principal **Menut Área Recreativa** (Wp.4 50M).

Crossing the road and the **Área Recreativa** car-park, we go behind the main building and the barbecue hut to follow a broad, trodden way descending between picnic tables (NW) to the small parking area at the bottom of the *Área Recreativa*. Bearing right, we take a broad, gated dirt track climbing towards **Puig Tomir**. Ignoring all minor branch tracks, we stay on this track as it meanders through mixed woodland, climbing through a series of concreted sections, eventually passing between two stone pillars to join the **Camí Vell de Pollença** (Wp.5 95M). Turning right, we follow the **Camí Vell** to the **Binifaldó Education Centre**, the large farmhouse visible for the last few minutes, where we emerge on the road to the **Binifaldó** bottling plant. Turning left, we follow the road up through an S-bend until it bears left through the bottling plant gates (Wp.6 110M), where we climb over the stone/concrete stile next to the closed gates on the right.

Ignoring the dirt track after the stile, we take the narrow path on the right (signposted 'Son Amer/Lluc'), which winds through the woods for fifteen minutes before rejoining the dirt track (Wp.7 125M). Bearing right, we climb to an unnamed, unmarked *coll* and continue on the dirt track down to **Coll Pelat** (Wp.8 135M). The GR continues on the level for **Lluc via Son Amer**, but we turn sharp right on a branch track descending toward the MA-10.

After an easy fifteen minute descent, we cross an immense ladder-stile over a fenced stone wall leading into the public **Menut** farm. Ignoring a branch 50 metres later, we continue straight ahead to go to the left of the farmhouse and rejoin the **Binifaldó** access lane, 250 metres from the MA-10. Turning left on the MA-10, we cross the road 75 metres later, just before the bend, and take a stony track (Wp.9 160M) gently descending between holm oak, olives and pine. Ignoring all subsequent branches, we follow this track for a little over fifteen minutes, rejoining the outward route at the wooden bridge behind the football field.

Despite its length, this circuit is relatively easy and only earns an exertion rating of 4 for the rock-hopping in the riverbed. The scenery is very varied, but the more remarkable variety is in what we walk in and on: roads, lanes, a paved pilgrims' way, concrete tracks, cart tracks, dirt tracks, cobbled paths, *carritx* covered ways, a limestone maze, the bed of a torrent… you name it, we walk it, excepting motorways and airport runways. The ascent on the **Camí Vell** from **Caimari** is easy and poses no difficulties. The descent, however, via the **Serra d'en Massot** torrent should not be undertaken in wet weather (there's little risk of flooding, but the rocks might be slippery). Pathfinding is a problem between Wps.17 & 21. Long trousers or pedal-pushers are preferable to shorts between Wps. 19 & 22. Start early to avoid the improbably large coaches that plough up and down the MA-2130.

4*   5½-6H **   20 km   550m / 550m   ↻   🍴 3

*   Short Versions 3
**   Short Versions **(a)** 2h   **(b)** 4h   **(c)** 2h (all estimated)

Short Versions	Stroll
(a) to **Lluc via Camí Vell**, returning by bus **(b)** bus to **Lluc** and descend via **Aucanella** **(c)** bus to **Lluc**, descend via **Camí Vell** (from the *fuente* at the top of the car-park)	Though it's a dreary slog at the end of a long walk, the lane between **Caimari** and **Binibona** might make a pleasant stroll on a fresh day. The **Carrer de Binibona** starts just below the smaller church at the top of **Caimari**.

Access: on foot from **Caimari** (accessible by bus). There's a large car-park on the MA-2130 at the northern end of **Caimari**. If two cars are available, you may wish to leave one at **Binibona** or the **Albellons Hotel**, thus avoiding the hot trudge along the tarmac at the end.

Camí Vell de Lluc

From the northern end of **Caimari** (Wp.1 0M), we follow the MA-2130 for 400 metres to the *mirador* at the first U-bend, where the **Camí Vell de Lluc** begins (Wp.2 5M). Climbing the broad track from the *mirador*, we bear right at a Y-junction (Wp.3 15M) on stairs leading to the main road, which we parallel for a while then cross (Wp.4 25M) to climb steeply on a newly paved section of the **Camí Vell**.

After passing the **Son Canta** farmhouse, we bear left (Wp.5 35M) on a new path descending alongside the road to the **Sa Coveta Área Recreativa**, where we go through a tunnel under the road (Wps.6 40M) and cross a stile to reach the start of a dirt track. We climb gently past a memorial to 'Isabel Morel Morro' (Wp.7 48M), then steeply to a junction where the main track, marked with a GR waypost, doubles back to the right (Wp.8 53M). Sticking with the GR and the steep climb, we cross a *coll* before descending to a signposted junction at the foot of a long, straight stretch of cobbling (Wp.9 70M). As you climb this cobbled stretch, it's worth looking down on the valley below us (SE). The small, wooded, conical mountain in the middle is **Puig Mitja**. Our return route is on the far side of this mountain.

The track narrows on a fully cobbled stretch climbing to a natural limestone gateway (Wp.10 85M) where it levels off before passing a large new building and, 20 metres later, a massive oak tree (Wp.11 90M). A gentle descent brings us to a crossroads of dirt tracks, where we maintain direction (NW) down to the main road (Wp.12 95M), 75 metres from the **Coll de sa Bataia** petrol station and bar/restaurant, where I suggest you take any refreshment you haven't got in your backpack: the coffee's not great, but the welcome is infinitely warmer than in the bars at **Lluc**.

50 metres north of the garage, we turn right on the road to **Lluc**. The **Camí Vell** descends to the left, but unless you have a strong compulsion to light a candle or catch a bus, there's little point going down to **Lluc** itself and I suggest you stay on the main road for 500 metres and, just after the first left-hand bend, take the GR-221 to the right, signposted 'Binifaldó/Pollença' (Wp.13 110M). N.B. this path joins the dirt track starting just before the bend, so you could take the dirt track immediately.

Thirty metres from the road, we bear right at a waypost and small bridge to cross a deforested area and join the dirt track from the gates. The track goes through a gap in a wall, where it narrows and starts to climb, crossing a watercourse before swinging round to join another track. Ignoring all branch tracks, we climb steadily, following the waypost, until the track dwindles to a path (Wp.14 130M), 100 metres after which we cross the **Coll de sa Font**, where there's another 'Binifaldó' signpost. 50 metres after the *coll*, we bear left on another dirt track leading to **Coll Pelat** and the branch track (Wp.15 140M) down to the **Menut** farmhouse (see Walk 29). Bearing right, we continue on the main dirt track, still following the GR, as it descends then climbs slightly to a third, unnamed *coll*. Descending steadily from the *coll*, we stay on the dirt track when the GR bears left onto a narrow path through the woods, and continue descending, soon coming onto a newly concreted stretch. The concrete gives way to partially gravelled dirt descending to a torrent and small bridge/ford, where the track swings left and starts climbing (Wp.16 155M). We leave the track just before the bridge/ford.

The cairn-marked route climbs slightly to the right, away from the torrent, but we descend into the torrent and start walking along its rocky bed, occasionally following a vague path along its right bank. The valley gradually narrows and the side-path eventually disappears under a rockspill, from where we are obliged to follow the bed of the torrent, hopping from rock to rock, occasionally steadying ourselves with our hands. After a little over twenty minutes, we pass two large, shady oaks, the second of which has a *sitja* underneath it. Sticking to the bed of the torrent, we pass through the remains of a wall, 10 metres after which, we bear left, leaving the stream bed on a broad path marked with two large cairns (Wp.17 190M).

One hundred metres later, we bear left on a very rough dirt track, which we leave after 50 metres, just after a short S-bend, bearing right and heading through the rocks to a line of oaks and a stone gateway (all that remains of an old wall) topped with a cairn. Going through the gateway, we wind along a natural path defined by outcrops of limestone, passing a large rock pond and crossing the rough dirt track twice, the second time beside a fragile looking waypost indicating 'Ses Figueroles/Binibona' on the right and 'Miner' on the left. Crossing the track and some low rocks, we follow a cairn-marked way winding through the rocks, bringing us down to the fenced fields of the recently restored **Aucanella** farmhouse, invisible at present but betrayed by a large bank of solar panels to our left. Pathfinding is tricky here, so follow the cairns carefully.

Just above the fenced fields, we bear right on an infinitesimally faint track (Wp.18 210M) for 50 metres, then left to find a faint path through a wall gateway (Wp.19 213M) running alongside a ditch next to the fields. At the end of the fields, we go through another wall gateway (Wp.20 217M) and bear left to cross the head of the **Torrent des Picarols** onto a faint path densely overgrown with *carritx* (watch out for concealed rocks). Passing behind a 5 metre high boulder, we bear right (S), staying on the level for about 100 metres, after which the path gradually starts to descend, passing occasional cairns.

The path passes a large stand of oaks (clearly visible from the top of the *torrent*), then runs alongside an old wall, before bearing away from the wall at a second stand of oaks and descending to a broader, clearer path (Wp.21 240M), about 250 metres south of the **Ses Figueroles** house, visible through

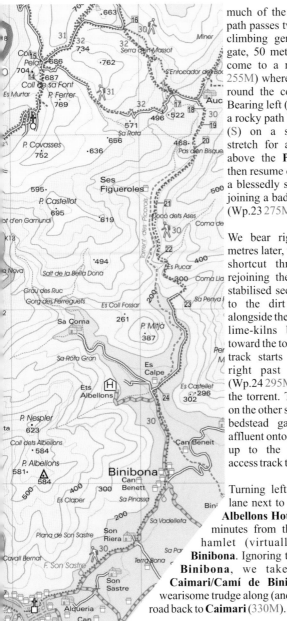

much of the descent. The clear path passes two gateways before climbing gently to a three-bar gate, 50 metres after which we come to a rocky pass (Wp.22 255M) where the views open up round the conical **Puig Mitja**. Bearing left (E), we zigzag down a rocky path before bearing right (S) on a slightly overgrown stretch for a final brief climb above the **Picarols** gorge. We then resume our descent, passing a blessedly shady stretch before joining a badly eroded cart track (Wp.23 275M).

We bear right, then left 100 metres later, where cairns mark a shortcut through the woods, rejoining the track on a better stabilised section. We now stick to the dirt track as it runs alongside the torrent, passing two lime-kilns before descending toward the torrent. Just before the track starts climbing, we turn right past two large cairns (Wp.24 295M) to cross the bed of the torrent. Taking a broad path on the other side, we go through a bedstead gate, then cross an affluent onto a cairn-marked path up to the partially asphalted access track to **Sa Coma**.

Turning left, we join a tarmac lane next to the driveway to the **Albellons Hotel**, a little under ten minutes from the implausibly tidy hamlet (virtually all hotels) of **Binibona**. Ignoring the main road out of **Binibona**, we take the **Carrer de Caimari/Camí de Binibona** for a rather wearisome trudge along (and sometimes up!) the road back to **Caimari** (330M).

Puig Tomir is not the most distinctive of Mallorca's summits, but does enjoy a unique perspective on **Pollença** and the **Formentor** peninsula. More importantly, the way up is a glorious, rough little climb with a distinctly Pyrenean feel to it. Add to that a leisurely descent and long loop through remote countryside, and you've got an offer you can't refuse. Don't be deceived by the brevity of the ascent, though. Although easy, it is a steep climb on rough ground and should not be undertaken by unaccompanied inexperienced walkers. Long trousers preferable between Wps.11 & 13.

* Short Versions   **(a)** 2h   **(b)** 1h40

Extension	Short Versions
From **Lluc** or **Menut** if Wp.1 is inaccessible (see text)	**(a)** if you don't mind the steep descent, return from the summit by the same route **(b)** from Wp.1 climb over the stone stile on your right and, ignoring the GR-path, follow the dirt track down till it bears sharp right at a concrete bridge/ford, Wp.16 of Walk 30. Follow Walk 30 till after Wp.17 where it emerges on the new track, joining this itinerary at Wp.14.

Access: by car or (starting from **Lluc** or the MA-10) bus (seasonal timetable)

We start from the gates of the **Binifaldó** bottling plant at the **Coll des Pedregaret** (Wp.1 0M) 2.9 km from the MA-10. NOTE: the main gates on the MA-10 are closed at weekends. If doing this walk at the weekend or arriving by bus, you can reach Wp.1 by any of the following four options:
(i) walk up the access road from km 17.4 of the MA-10 (quickest option);
(ii) follow the GR-221 from **Lluc** (most logical for the return);
(iii) follow Walk 29 from Lluc (longest and most attractive);
(iv) follow Walk 29 from the *Menut Área Recreativa* (Wp.4 of Walk 29) (short and attractive).

Taking the path to the right of the bottling plant gates, we climb alongside the fence before bearing right for a steeper climb through the woods, following cairns and red waymarks. Above the woods, we cross a scree-filled gully (Wp.2 15M) and descend briefly before climbing to traverse the head of a broader scree slope. At the north-eastern tip of the scree slope, we bear right up a second narrow gully, passing a steel cable set in the rock as a handrail, and emerging midway along another scree-filled gully (Wp3 30M). After climbing straight up this third gully, we scramble up a 5 metre high rockface (Wp.4 40M) with the help of two metal hoops and another steel cable - if this sounds alarming, bear in mind it has been tested in accordance with The Old English Sheepdog Trial (see Walk 22). We then follow a long curving valley for 50 metres before bearing right on a cairn-marked path climbing to a clear breach in the rock defining the valley.

After the breach, we continue climbing (SE) for 150 metres, following cairns onto the ridge (55M) from where we have clear views of the southern plain

Puig Tomir

and **Alcúdia Bay**. Bearing left (another path on the left lower down can also be taken), we follow the ridge (NE) soon coming into view of the summit and its trig point (NOT the small summit with a pole at the top of the curving valley). Following the cairns across largely pathless limestone brings us back into sight of **Puigs Roig** and

Caragoler de Femenia on our left (Wp.5 65M), after which a gentle climb on rough ground leads to the summit (Wp.6 75M) from where we have superb views down the **Pollença** valley. Behind **Pollença**, the first small hump is **Serra de la Coma**, the sharp peak is the **Cuculla de Fartatrix**, and the large block-like mountain below us is **Puig de Ca**, our next objective.

classic rockscape below Puig Tomir

First though, we descend to the **Casa Neu** or **Snow House**, clearly visible to the south-east, where there is a grassy windbreak tucked behind the snow-gatherers' cabin (Wp.7 80M). Beyond the cabin there's a splendid snow-pit, 20 metres to the right of which, a red arrow and cairns indicate our way down. Following the cairns, red dots and occasional stretches of path, we descend in a south-easterly direction before bearing left (NNE).

A steady descent leads to a large grey metal post (Wp.8 100M) where we leave the clear trail and turn sharp right, following the cairns to scramble down onto the western limit of the **Coll del Puig de Ca**. Crossing the *coll* (E) we join a faint track (Wp.9 115M) near the wall climbing from the far side of the *coll* to the *puig*.

Turning right, we follow the track over a grassy rise, where it starts descending, skirting the fenced depression of **Clot Fondo** and running into a better-stabilised, partially concreted track down to the **Coll de l'Arena** junction (Wp.10 135M), visible for most of our descent from Wp.9. Bearing right, we follow the main track across the broad plain of **Camp Redo**. When the track ends in a turning circle (Wp.11 145M), we head for a large ladder-stile and a gap in the fence. Beyond the fence, a narrow path winds through large clumps of *carritx* (SW) passing occasional cairns and crossing the odd outcrop of rock, making its way to the head of a narrow valley (Wp.12 165M), at the top of which there are numerous pleasant picnic spots. We meander through the valley, following cairns when the path disappears in the undergrowth, before descending to pass under two large oaks, 100 metres after which we come to a new fence and ladder-stile (Wp.13 185M).

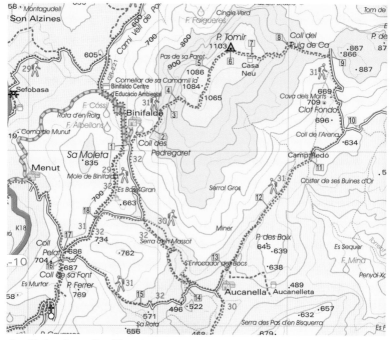

fungi below Serra d'en Massot

Crossing the stile, we follow a broad stony trail leading to a dirt track behind the **Aucanella** (AKA **Alcanella**) farmhouse (invisible on this route).

Bearing right, we follow the track, crossing another new fence and stile, 100 metres after which we cross the signposted path taken in Walk 30. We can either follow the signposts or continue along the track as it winds round to a flat area with a ruined shelter sandwiched between the rocks on our left. Leaving the flat area, the track climbs slightly through an S-bend, just after which there's a large oak (Wp.14 200M).

At this point we intersect with Walks 30 & 32, and can return to **Binifaldo** via the torrent featured in Walk 30, the off path-route of Walk 32, or (recommended) the end of Walk 32. For a description of this route, see Walk 32 Wps.7-11. Walk 32 Wps.8-11 have been appended to the waypoint file of the present itinerary.

Though two thirds of this walk is on paths featured elsewhere, the new third is so very enjoyable, I reckoned it merited an itinerary number of its own. Gratifyingly, it is the result of a happy chance. Too often when a researcher tries to 'invent' new routes unpublished elsewhere, the big fool will discover all too soon precisely why they are unpublished, often as not ending up floundering about in banks of gorse and hanging off precipices with the dawning realization that this really isn't a whole heap of fun. In this instance, though, the opposite was the case. Setting out to check the middle sections of Walks 30 & 31, we saw some cairns, wondered where they lead (as one does), and discovered this glorious trail traversing the **Serra d'en Massot**, an unassuming little rise sandwiched between the massifs of **Tomir** and **Massanella**. It's a fabulous offpath route, wellmarked with cairns and blue waymarks, that is ideal for getting off the beaten track without risk to life, limb or overall reserves of oomph.

Access: by car or (starting from **Lluc** see Walk 31 for ways to reach the start on foot) by bus

mossy oak

Starting from the gates of the **Binifaldo** bottling plant (only accessible by car on working days) (Wp.1 0M), we cross the stonestepped stile, as if following the GR to **Lluc**, then immediately leave the GR, taking the broad dirt track descending to the south through attractive, moss mantled woodland. After a

off path

steady descent, the track swings sharp right at a small bridge/ford (Wp.16 of Walk 30) (Wp.2 15M). Walk 30 descends into the bed of the torrent at this point, but for the present itinerary, we maintain our southerly direction on a cairnmarked path forking off the track and climbing above the right bank of the torrent.

After crossing a small rise, the path dips down and disappears amid rough rock. On the far side of the dip, we climb onto a limestone shoulder where cairns and blue waymarks indicate the start of the offpath section. There are patches of path along the flank of the mountain, but for the most part we're picking our way across a fabulous rockscape of rough limestone, where some of the karstic erosion is so delicate it appears to have been sculpted by a designing hand or to be the fossilized remains of some convoluted invertebrate.

sculpted by a designing hand

You don't really need to consult the book here, but maintaining a southwesterly direction, we go through an open gateway in a fence thirty metres after the disappearance of the path (Wp.3 24M).

As the views over the **Aucanella** valley open out fully, we descend briefly, then follow a contour passing a stony *sitja* (Wp.4 31M) before descending again alongside the foot of a sloping outcrop of rock. 100 metres after a second stone cloaked *sitja*, we pass below a large solitary oak (Wp.5 44M) from where we weave our way through the *carritx* to the bed of the torrent (Wp.17 of Walk 30) (Wp.6 46M). Crossing the torrent, we follow a clear path (SE) to join a stony track less than 100 metres later, where we turn right (Wp.7).

The track traverses a wilderness of spurge, mastic and scrubby holm oak then climbs steadily before dwindling to a trail (Wp.8 61M), which continues to climb briefly alongside a tumbledown wall before dipping back into dense woodland. The trail climbs through the woods, broadening to a rough forestry track which we follow until it joins the GR at a wayposted junction (Wp.9 81M), where we turn right.

We now simply follow the GR back to **Binifaldo**, forking right at a Y-junction of tracks (Wp.10 82M) and left above an S-bend (Wp.11 91M), to end with an agreeable stroll on a sinuous footpath winding through the woods.

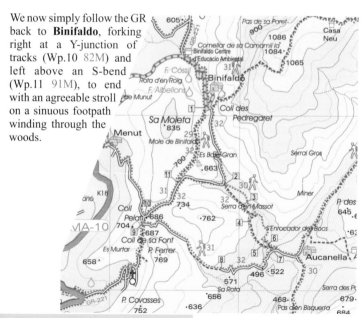

a. Puig de Maria

Puig de María

Don't be fooled by the insignificant looking little squiggle representing this walk on the map, nor by the fact that most of it is on a road. This is a glorious little excursion, ideal on a blustery winter's day when it would be unwise to tackle a wilder landscape. Our objective is the **Santuari de la Mare de Deu des Puig**, home to various religious houses from 1348 to 1988, nowadays a bar-restaurant-refuge.

3 | 1H 10M* | 4 km | 300m / 300m | ⟺ | 5

Access: on foot from **Pollença**.

* return, + 30M for exploring

We start at km 52 of the MA-2200, also the **Pollença** by-pass, on a tarmac lane signposted 'Puig de Maria' (Wp.1 0M). If starting on foot from **Pollença**, find the Repsol petrol station (signposted throughout the town as 'Benzinera'), then take the cul-de-sac to the right of the Renault concession and cut across the wasteland onto a lane that leads to a derelict house in front of Wp.1. Following the tarmac lane, we bear right after 100 metres, from where we already have fine views of the higher mountains behind **Pollença**. After climbing steadily for ten minutes, the tarmac gives way to concrete and we pass the green gates of the last house.

Ignoring the water-erosion 'shortcuts' (the road is steep enough), we continue climbing through mixed woodland, passing occasional red crosses daubed on the trees - waymarks for pilgrims, not walkers. The road ends (Wp.2 25M) in a tiny turning circle (room for three small cars, but usually full) and we continue on the restored, neatly cobbled, donkey trail with fine views south towards **Puig de Sant Martí** (see Walk 41). One hundred metres before the sanctuary, we ignore a signposted turning to the left (our return route). At the sanctuary, we can either bear right to go directly to the chapel or continue left of the main walls and go through its *Área Recreativa* (Wp.3 35M) to the impressive refectory. In either case, it's worth spending half an hour exploring. For once, what man has done with it is as magnificent and harmonious as the site: this is no dank cell for a solitary anchorite, nor an intimidating symbol of authority, but a superbly designed, well-proportioned building that once housed up to seventy people. A drink in the bar is almost compulsory. Taking the path to the left of the *Área Recreativa*, the **Camí dels Ermitans**, we visit the ruined *torre* (**Mirador de Coll Vell**) and the fenced grotto (**Avenc del Mare de Deu**), before circling back to rejoin the donkey trail for our descent.

b. Fonts de Ufanes

The **Fonts de Ufanes** are ephemeral springs that flow after prolonged perioc of heavy rain in the highlands (to check if they're in spate, call 900151617 However, water is not the only attraction to this tiny itinerary. The woods c the **Gabelli** estate, where the springs are situated and which has recently bee purchased by the government, are so enchanting that this is a lovely stro even without the fonts. Ideal when it's too hot or too overcast to venture int the mountains. Apart from the diversion up the torrent, the itinerary is clearl wayposted throughout.

Access: by car

charcoal burners' hut

We start from the picturesqu chapel of **Sant Miguel** to th east of **Campanet** on the Car Vell de Pollen a (Wp.1 0M Strolling back to the road, w follow the Cami Vell for 7 metres to a tiny wooden gar giving pedestrian access to th **Gabelli** estate (Wp.2 2M where a broad track travers

an idyllic pastoral landscape.

Taking the left fork at a Y-junction (Wp.3 10M), we soon leave the grazing land and enter the woods, which are some of the loveliest in the public domain. Immediately after passing a particularly fine reconstruction of a charcoal burner's hut, we fork right at a Y-junction (the branch on the left ends at locked gates a couple of hundred metres later) (Wp.4 20M) to approach a large *casa foresta*l that functions as an information centre.

Just after the *casa forestal*, a fork off to the left (Wp.5 24M) takes us past th tumbledown remains of a *talaiot* (a neolithic stone dwelling) to reach th **Torrent de Biniatro** (AKA sa Mina) (Wp.6 26M). If the torrent's dry and th rocks aren't too slippery, it's worth walking along the stream bed for 25 metres to the dam wall defining the estate (Wp.7). It is possible to scrambl over the embankment on the right of the dam to access the **Biniatro** estate, bu the fences suggest you're not really meant to do this! Instead, we simply retur to Wp.5 and follow the wayposted loop out of the woods to rejoin our outwar route at Wp.3.

A perfect combination of easy walking and wild landscape, the **Havanor** track behind the **Mortitx** estate is very possibly the finest stroll on the island. Our previous version of this itinerary followed the track right to the end and then a little bit more, and it had been my intention to extend the itinerary for the new edition by trail-blazing an off-path descent to **Rafal d'Ariant** and the bottom of the **Mortitx** gorge. However, readers' reports have suggested that the original access restrictions designed to protect the resident Black Vultures during the breeding season are gradually being extended, prohibiting walkers from passing the **Coll d'es Vent or** even, in one instance, the **Torrent de Comes**. When we re-walked the route in 2008, there was no evidence of these restrictions (notwithstanding the fact that one reader had actually sent us a photo of the signboard outlining them!), however, we felt it best to limit ourselves to the signposted route to the new **Havanor Refuge**, on the assumption that a public picnic spot will probably remain accessible. The walk is considerably shorter than it was, but no matter. It could become even shorter and still remain a gem. For uptodate news on when and where you can go, check with the **Tramuntana Information Centre** at **Lluc**.

Access: by car or bus (request stop). There's adequate roadside parking at the farm gates and 50 metres down the road.

From the **Mortitx** farm gates at km10.8 of the MA10 (Wp.1 0M), we follow the driveway track as it passes a tennis court and the main farmhouse, after which it descends to the left, passing the estate winery before reaching a Y-junction at a corner of the principal vineyard (Wp.2 8M), where we fork right for the 'Refugi'.

rock 'chimney'

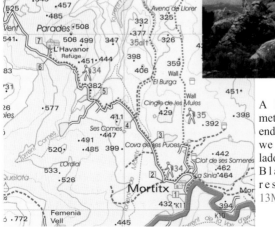

A little over 400 metres later, at the end of the vineyard, we cross a high ladder stile into the Black Vulture reserve (Wp.3 13M).

We now traverse a classic Mallorcan rockscape dotted with tormented olive, oleaster, and carob trees, the rocks and trees conspiring in their convolutions like weird sisters in an ancient fable. 400 metres into the reserve, we pass a narrow, cairnflanked turning on the right into the **Mortitx Gorge** (Wp.4), a worthwhile detour if you don't intend doing Walk 35.

dam wall

After climbing through a concrete bend, we come to a major Y-junction (Wp.5 28M). The track on the left climbs to the upper dam on the **Torrent de Comes**, a ten minute diversion that is also worthwhile, especially if access is restricted further along the **Havanor** track. For the main walk however, we fork right to cross the lower dam wall and climb along a surfaced track toward a distinctive chimney of rock.

overlooking the Mortitx gorge from the Havanor track

200 metres after the rock chimney, we fork right (Wp.6 40M) to descend to the **Havanor** refuge (Wp.7 43M), which is locked but has a pleasant picnic table, a stoop for shelter, and a chemical toilet tucked around the back. We return by the same route.

Havanor refuge

35 RAFAL D'ARIANT & MORTITX GORGE

This is the famous twin of the preceding itinerary, a descent into the wild, untenanted land around the abandoned **Rafal d'Ariant** farmhouse. Pathfinding is difficult and the looped return via the **Mortitx Gorge** is only for the adventurous. If you're short of time and value views over sweat sodden T-shirts and hard walking, Walk 34 is a better bet. If you want to be in the heart of the wilderness, this is the walk for you. If you have time for both, the two itineraries complement each other and are both highly recommended

4*   3½ H **   9.5 km   400m   400m   0

*   linear, 5 if returning via the gorge
**   + 1h for exploring the **Ariant** estate, Short Version 2h20

Extensions: see text.

Stroll
Take the **l'Havanor** track and turn right at Wp.15 (look for a cairn on the right 5 minutes after Wp.2 of Walk 34) to the head of the gorge.

Access: by car or bus (request stop).

We start from the **Mortitx** farm gates (Wp.1 0M) as per Walk 34. Behind the tennis courts, we ignore a first turning on the right to a tiny bungalow, and take the second right passing a waymarked hut. The track descends between former cherry orchards (most of the trees have recently been uprooted) before veering right then left through a wall - if this is blocked, there's a stile just after the track veers right. We then bear left at a Y-junction and leave the track 30 metres later, turning right on a stony path (Wp.2 10M) badly overgrown with *carritx*. GPS owners who have been mocked as gadget-geeks, can now have their revenge: most of the waypoints on the outward route, are for you.

Winding through the *carritx* and picking our way over outcrops of rock, we pass occasional waymarks and cairns, descending into a large depression dotted with pine trees. If you intend coming back the same way, it's worth glancing back every once in a while to orient yourself for the return. After a gradual descent, we cross a broken fence beside a stile (Wp.3 20M) and continue on a slightly clearer path alongside the fence. Ignoring branches to the right, we cross a low stone retaining wall (Wp.4 25M) and continue alongside the remains of the fence. We then cross another wall, either by a high stile or through a broken gate on the left (Wp.5 30M) into the **Ariant** estate.

Maintaining direction (NNE), we climb through the rocks directly ahead of the stile, where there's a red waymark. Following occasional cairns and waymarks, and even more occasional stretches of clear path, we continue winding through the *carritx* and rocks (NE), and start descending through a <u>very</u> overgrown stretch - though given the prevailing invasion of *carritx*, it would be simpler to distinguish the 'undergrown' patches. If you haven't got a GPS, look for the cairns. In a landscape of rocks and rocks and rocks, and *carritx* and *carritx* and *carritx*, cairns are a better guide than words.

Rough walking, occasionally using our hands to lower ourselves between rocks, brings us down to what appears to be a natural descent off to the left. It may be natural, but it ain't for us. We climb to the right, as indicated by blue and yellow waymarks on a large cairn-topped rock (Wp.6 45M), maintaining our general direction (NNE) for 50 metres before bearing left (NNW) up a rocky escarpment to a large cairn on a broad, flat rock. Continuing on the level, we pass above a shallow depression and another natural-not-for-us descent to the left.

Maintaining direction (ENE), we climb above the depression (Wp.7 55M) and briefly follow a very faint path before climbing steeply (NNE) up a rocky watershed to a yellow arrow, where we bear left onto a *coll* with clear views of the sea (Wp.8 60M).

The way becomes slightly clearer as we descend to cross what must once have been a small lagoon and is now a *carritx* covered cirque. Winding through the *carritx*, we climb briefly before resuming our descent and coming into view of the **Rafal d'Ariant** plain. After passing an old sign for 'Mortitx', we bear left and descend steeply, soon coming into view of the **Rafal d'Ariant** farmhouse. We then zigzag down below marvellously eroded cliffs to the house (Wp.9 90M).

There are at least four extensions possible from the farmhouse:

(1) peeking over the cliffs to the north (quite sickening if you suffer from vertigo);
(2) peering into the mouth of the **Cova de ses Buixes**, or **Witches' Cave**, which is the standard end to this walk;
(3) descending for a bathe (when the water's calm) at the **Caleta d'Ariant**; or
(4) in fine weather, exploring the **Torrent Fondo de Mortitx**, which is the start of the alternative return via the gorge.

For the first three, we take the clearly visible but occasionally overgrown path to the east of the house down to a small spring with an arched roof. After the spring, we head for the **Musclo de ses Cordes**, the massive cave-riddled bluff to the north-east, crossing two walls and the dry bed of the torrent.

... dramatic views en route ...

(1) To peek over the cliffs (15M return from the house), we leave the path 100 metres after the torrent and bear left, crossing flat pathless land to the rock shelf where the torrent used to spill into a waterfall.

(2) For the cave and the cove, we stay on the path to cross a broad pass behind the **Musclo de ses Cordes**. The path descends a shallow gully of reddish-brown rocks, passing a large rock, walled-in as a makeshift shelter (easily missed on the descent). Five metres before a massive overhanging rock with a partial wall (Wp.10 a little over fifteen minutes from the house), cairns mark a faint way across the rocks to the left, at the end of which (10M return from Wp.10) a shelf over a precipitous drop gives us a view of the entrance to the **Witches' Cave**.

(3) For the cove (15M return from Wp.10), we continue past the overhanging rock and follow the cairns for a very rough descent down to the *caleta*. <u>Do not swim here if there's a swell</u>. This extension is only for those who will do anything for a swim: it's a rough descent onto sharp volcanic rock that's murder on bare feet, though there's a nice ledge for rock bathing.

(4) To explore the **Torrent Fondo de Mortitx** and start the alternative return; take the rough path to the south-west of the house, passing a series of dead fig trees and running alongside a dry watercourse. Shortly after two large pine trees, we come to the torrent where there are various waymarks (Wp.11, 5M from the house). 100 metres to the right, under a tower of rock, a series of shallow pools lead up to one deep, permanent pool. Unfortunately, it's not really swimmable as access is difficult and the water's a bit scummy. Either return the same way or take the…

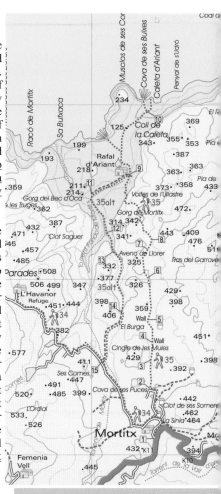

Alternative return
Rafal d'Ariant is wild; the **Mortitx Gorge** is very, very wild and potentially very dangerous. There's no path, just lots of energetic scrambling. Only recommended for those who are happy without any sign of civilisation apart from intermittent cairns and waymarks. <u>Do not venture into the gorge after rain or if there's a risk of rain.</u> <u>Do tell somebody where you're going</u>.

Turning left at Wp.11 (0M), we follow the riverbed, hopping and scrambling from rock to rock. As we climb across a rock slope to the right of a first pool, the gorge starts to narrow and deepen. After ten minutes, we come to a second pool, where we either have to get wet or gingerly edge our way across the shelving rock on the left. Less than two minutes after this second pool, we have a choice; our only one of the ascent so don't mess it up or you'll get into hellish difficulties further up! At an obvious fork in the gorge, we take the cairn and waymarked affluent to the <u>left</u> (Wp.12 12M).

Having made the correct choice, we hop from rock to rock up the affluent, absolved of responsibility for pathfinding – almost. After a particularly wild and narrow stretch where we have to constantly lever ourselves up with our hands between rocks, we come to a red waymark and yellow painted '30' mins (Wp.13 25M). Ignoring a rough path climbing towards a cave on the left, we carry straight on towards a cairn, after which a bilious green waymark indicates the onward route along the watercourse. The gorge gradually widens between towering rock pinnacles and we pass the occasional comforting cairn – it's not that you can get lost, but it's nice to know somebody's been here before you.

After an exhausting scramble, the gorge opens out into a natural sloping amphitheatre (40M). Following a faint path bearing right, we climb to the amphitheatre's southern 'gate', a massive rock with cliffs towering on either side (Wp.14 50M). To the left of the rock, a rough path and a final rocky stretch bring us to the base of a cliff, where we bear right on a clear path leading out of the gorge. Crossing a broken fence (60M), we stroll along a level dirt path that soon crosses a dry torrent, almost immediately after which we go through an olive grove to join the l'Havanor dirt track (Wp.15 65M). Turning left, we follow this track back past the Mortitx vineyard and farm buildings to the start of the walk (85M).

The **Bóquer Valley** is a bird watcher's paradise, but most visitors are lured by its unspoiled beauty and a walk that's suitable for all but the most resolutely sedentary holidaymakers. It can be crowded, but it's no less beautiful for that, and if it's solitude you're after, take the extension - nobody's going to be following you up there!

The Bóquer Valley

The mass migration of birds begins in April, but there are notable sightings for 'twitchers' all year round, in particular the rare Audouin Gull, which is found only in the Balearics and Turkey.

| 2* | 1½-2H ** | 6 km | 160m *** 160m | ⟺ | 0 |

*   Short Version 1, Extension 5
**   + 1h05 for the extension, Short Version 1h-1h15
***   Short Version 80 metres, Extension + 270 metres

Short Version To **Coll del Moro**	**Stroll** To Wp.2, returning via the alternative path.	**Additional stroll** The **Bosquet de Bóquer**, 300 metres from Wp.1 along the **Formentor** road.	**Extension Cavall Bernat** (see text)

Access: on foot from **Port de Pollença**

To reach the start on foot, we follow **Port de Pollença** esplanade (NNE) to the **Restaurante Los Pescadores** and turn left on **Avenguda de Bocchoris**, crossing **Carrer de Formentor** to a pine and tamarisk-flanked promenade, the **Área Pública Bóquer**, **Camí de Bóquer** (Wp.1 0M) (signposted from the new bypass to Formentor if arriving by car).

At the end of the **Camí de Bóquer**, formerly the driveway to the **Bóquer** farm (the castellated building ahead of us), we cross the road and take the **Predio Bóquer** track up to the farm gates, where we are greeted by the customary catalogue of prohibitions.

Going through the main gates, we pass in front of the house, go through a second gate, and bear right through a third gate (the Mallorcans do love a good gate!), after which we follow the broad path climbing gently between the **Serra del Cavall Bernat** and the **Creveta Ridge**.

Going through a narrow defile formed by two pinnacles of rock, we pass a lime-kiln within sight of a small stand of pine, after which the valley broadens and the outline of the bay becomes clearer. The path crosses a stone wall

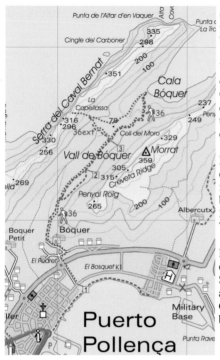

(Wp.2 20M), just before which a branch track doubles back on the right.

Up to our left, we can see one of the 'eyes' through the **Cavall Bernat**. The shallow dip in the ridge to the right of the eye is **La Capellassa**, our objective on the extension.

For the present though, we continue towards the sea and, five minutes later, reach a branch path on the left (Wp.3 25M) marked by a large cairn. This is the extension.

If you're not doing the extension
Stay on the main path for another five minutes to the **Coll del Moro**, identifiable by a large pile of stones.

For the short version
Stop at the *coll* and return via the same route or the alternative stroll.

For the full version
Bear right at the *coll* and follow the cairns down the valley along a wide path that reaches the beach fifteen minutes later. The beach itself isn't up to much, stony, speckled with patches of tar, and strewn with piles of flotsam, but the bay is unspoilt and the water's good for swimming in fine weather, though hazardous in rough seas due to the rocks and debris.

Extension
The scramble up to **La Capellassa** on the **Cavall Bernat** is nigh on indescribable, but if you've got sturdy legs and a hunger for stunning views, it's a must. Turning left at Wp.2, we descend a rough but clear path beside a stone wall, at the end of which we start climbing. The path becomes increasingly difficult to distinguish from other patches of bare ground, but following the cairns we climb to the right of a smooth outcrop of rock. The cairns are confusing here, so bear in mind you're not going anywhere specific and where you are going is up all the way!

As we near **La Capellassa**, the path clears briefly before disappearing again. In the last 50 metres, various routes splinter off from one another, the main cairn-marked route bearing left toward the **Cavall Bernat** proper. It is possible to follow the ridge all the way to **Cala St. Vicenç**, but this is notoriously difficult and not recommended. Instead, we bear right, straight up a pathless slope aiming for the lowest point on the ridge. But don't hurry. There's a sheer drop on the far side and it's not one to confront suddenly. If the route up was indescribable, so are the views from the top, taking in the jagged grandeur of **Formentor** to the east and toe-curling cliffs to the west.

A forty minute climb is followed by a twenty-five minute descent along the same route, picking our way from cairn to cairn with extreme caution since it's very unstable underfoot. However, instead of bearing right towards Wp.3, we bear left halfway down to follow goat paths towards the bay, emerging 50 metres north-west of **Coll del Moro** on a minor path, where we bear left for a gentle descent to a boulder-strewn watercourse leading to the beach.

To return, we climb between the remains of old walls 10 metres east of the watercourse. Joining the main cairn-marked path, we wind up the eastern side of the valley, passing ancient terracing walls and an old *canaleta* outlet, reaching the **Coll del Moro** fifteen minutes later.

For a slight variation on the return and for the stroll
Bear left at Wp.2 (5M from **Coll del Moro**) on a broad track climbing slightly towards **Penyal Roig**. The track flattens out and dwindles to a path in front of a concrete hut with a green door, before dropping down below a narrow stone-capped *canaleta* to rejoin the outward route just short of the defile.

Cap Formentor doesn't have a great reputation for walking, as its sheer cliffs and rough rocks can seem a little daunting when seen from the road. And if the mania for fencing continues apace, this sorry reputation will become sorrier still, which is a pity because there are some excellent walks in the area, as these Creek & Peak combinations are designed to illustrate. The traditional circuit of **Na Blanca** has been blocked near the main **Formentor** car-park and, at the time of writing, one version of the southern ascent is overgrown. However, the main route is still passable. It's tough walking over rough virtually pathless terrain and, though it's carefully marked with cairns, you need reasonable pathfinding skills. But the views from the top are worth the effort: 'limpid blue waters', 'dramatic crags', 'fabulous vistas' – you trundle them out, the clichés all fit.

N.B. This route is not recommended after heavy rains as the 'path' at Wp.2, already a scramble, becomes a watercourse, making it difficult to negotiate.

* at **Playa Formentor**
Access: by car and bus (from **Alcúdia** & **Port de Pollença**)

Stroll	Additional Stroll
Along the beach to 'the poets'.	From the **Mirador d'es Colomer** on the MA-2210 to the **Albercutx** watchtower (also possible by car).

From the recreation area directly behind **Formentor** beach (Wp.1 0M), we cross the restaurant terrace and stroll along the beach for ten minutes, passing below the long, low white buildings of the hotel. Approaching **Illa de Formentor**, we climb onto a large turning circle in front of the **Club de los Poetas**, which despite the name and uniformed maid, is not a club and probably has very little to do with poetry, either.

Following the road inland, we pass a branch to the right and the deliriously pompous **Castillo del Mar**, after which the road bears sharp left round the hotel tennis courts, and we continue on a lane off to the right marked with a dead-end sign.

Na Blanca

We follow this lane through successive tarmac and concrete sections until it ends at the green gates of the last house, on the left of which a red waymark indicates the start of our scramble up to **Na Blanca** (Wp.2 30M).

Guided by cairns and the occasional waymarks, we zigzag up to join the remains of an old path climbing the ridge (NNE) from a gate at the back of the house.

After twenty minutes, the path loses what little definition it had and we follow the cairns, climbing steadily through scattered pine and dwarf palm with increasingly fine views to the east.

As the gradient eases, we bear WNW, picking our way across jagged debris within sight of the white rocks of the peak, which is in fact still surprisingly far away. Although the way seems simple, keep following the cairns as this is very rough walking and the marked route has not been chosen by accident. Halfway along this westerly ridge, beware of cairns indicating a way to the right. We maintain direction to skirt the cliffs overlooking the hotel and finally reach the top (Wp.3 80M). The return by the same route takes about an hour, plus however long you need for bathing from the pretty little sandy beach in front of 'the poets'.

The first part of this little known itinerary, an easy stroll down to **Cala Figuera**, is suitable for a family excursion. The climb to **El Morro de Catalunya** is not, and should only be attempted by experienced walkers. It's not technically difficult, but does cross rough, pathless ground and involves picking one's way from cairn to cairn, hoping the people who built them knew what they were doing - they did, as it happens, but it's not always evident. The rewards, though, are correspondingly great as we climb into some of the wildest terrain encountered anywhere on the island and enjoy a unique view of the peninsula. Don't do it on your own, or when it's wet or very windy.

| 5 | ⌚ (3-3½ H) * | ⟹ 8.5 km | ⋀ | ↗ 380m ↘ 380m | ⟺ | 🍴 0 |

*   Short Version 1½h

| **Short Version** To the *coll* at Wp.3 | **Stroll** To **Cala Figuera** |

Access: by car

Cap Formentor

We start at km 12 of the MA-2210 to **Cap Formentor**, parking next to the road just after the milepost or on a rough dirt track on the right 50 metres further along. From a gateway in the fence on the northern side of the road (Wp.1 0M), we cross a clearing to take a broad dirt track bearing right.

The track descends to a platform above the beach, where it joins our return route, the steep path down from the large parking area at km 13. Bearing left, we take the steps down to the stony beach (Wp.2 20M), which was a bit smelly when we passed, littered with the decaying corpses of tiny blue jellyfish, but there are nice rock-bathing shelves below the rock sheets along the northern side of the bay, at the end of which we can peer into a remarkable sea-cave.

For the full and short versions
We bear left at the end of the rock sheets and climb towards a clear gully, where we find a red waymark and cairned trails climbing on either side of the gully. Ignoring the cairns on the left, we cross the bottom of the gully and follow the cairns to the right, climbing alongside the rocky outcrop on the gully's left bank (our right). Edging up the rock, we pass a large uprooted pine tree and climb to the right of a second small outcrop of rock bringing us into view of the lighthouse at **Cap Formentor**. Following the cairns, we climb along a rockspill to pass behind the second outcrop of rock, back into the gully.

The cairns briefly disappear, but up to our right, a red waymark on a rock flanked by dwarf palm indicates where we cross onto the gully's right bank.

Following a route well marked with cairns, we climb steadily to the obvious *coll* north of the gully (Wp.3 55M) though strictly speaking it's not really a *coll*, since you wouldn't want to pass onto the other side, where there are almost sheer drops down to the sea.

Even if you don't intend continuing to the end, it's worth climbing to this point. The views of **Cala Figuera** and **El Fumat** are superb, while the outlook to the north would curdle milk, let alone blood.

For the full walk

We bear right at the *coll* towards another cairn and a waymark indicating that we climb straight up the steep, exposed rock just to the right of the cliffs (yes, <u>that</u> way up!). At first, there's no confirmation that this is the right route, but we soon pass two small cairns (invisible from below) and climb very steeply to a tall cairn in the pine trees at the top of the slope (Wp.4 60M).

We've now done most of the climbing, but the roughest ground and most tortuous pathfinding awaits.

Casas Velles

Beforehand though it's worth looking back inland, where the views are already opening out and we can see the green fields of **Casas Velles** and, in the distance, the **Torre de Albercutx**.

Bearing slightly left from the tall cairn, we climb for 10 metres to another cairn and the first of several red arrows that guide us along the crest. The first arrow indicates our more or less level way round the edge of the first outcrop of rock.

After 50 metres, at a cairn and waymark, we bear sharp left to climb steeply for 15 metres, after which we bear right again to resume our general north-easterly direction. Climbing gently, we pass a second red arrow, 10 metres after which a third red arrow directs us <u>downhill</u>.

Descending over large smooth rocks for 5 metres (on your bottom if necessary, this is no place for dignity), we bear left at a fourth arrow to skirt a pine tree and pass a fifth arrow indicating the way over the smooth exposed rock, beyond which we climb back towards the crest along a route marked by cairns and waymarks.

The next red arrow (Number Six if I haven't missed any) indicates a way directly over the rocks, while the cairns lead round to the right of the rocks: <u>follow the cairns</u>. Carefully picking our way round the southern side of the rocks (not dangerous, but the rocks are sharp and a fall would be very unpleasant), we rejoin the waymarked route and scramble over the rocks onto a broad ridge, which we follow for 100 metres to the large pile of stones on the top (Wp.5 95M) from where we have a matchless view of the peninsula.

We return by the same route. The descent back to the creek takes a little over an hour, after which a swim is not so much welcome as essential.

To return to the starting point
From the platform above the beach, we take the narrow, overgrown path climbing SSW. Just before the pine trees halfway up, we bear right onto another overgrown path and keep climbing (W) at each junction till the path broadens, first to a walking trail then a forest track, joining the main road five minutes from Wp.1.

39 CREEK & PEAK 3 - UNNAMED SUMMIT & NA BLANCA from CALA MURTA

Apart from the last stretch, this is an easy walk along tarmac lanes and dirt tracks. Though blighted by a big, ugly house, **Cala Murta** is an easily accessible, attractive creek with a stony beach and small picnic area. The unnamed summit enjoys fine views and is adjacent to **Na Blanca**, an extension avoiding most of the pathfinding problems of Walk 37. Though not as wild as the other creek-&-peak walks, this is a pleasant excursion with some excellent views.

* + 20M for the extension	**Stroll** To **Cala Murta/El Castellet** and back.
** + 80 metres for the extension	**Extension** To **Na Blanca** (see text).

Access: by car. Park at the large car-park at km13 of the MA-2210 above **Cala Figuera**.

We start shortly before km 13 of the MA-2210 at a walking sign for **Cala Murta** (Wp.1 0M) indicating the tarmac lane down to the creek. The attractive little lane winds through a profusion of *pistacia* and dwarf palms to pass a transformer tower and start its gentle descent. After passing a picnic area on our left and a first branch track on our right, we cross a small bridge over the dry torrent, just after which there is a second branch on the right (15M Wp.3), the track we follow for the full walk.

For the moment though, we continue on the tarmac lane, which ends at the gates of a private house. Bearing right on the dirt access track, we cross the beach (20M) to a signposted path west of the creek, which leads to a small *mirador* above the rocky headland at **El Castellet** (Wp.2 25M) from where we have attractive views along the coast in both directions.

Retracing our steps to the branch beside the torrent (Wp.3 35M), we take the broad dirt track running alongside the torrent. The track soon passes a *sitja* and dips down to cross an affluent just below a small dam wall, from where it bears left to climb alongside the affluent, gently at first then more steadily, until it comes to a locked gate.

In theory, this land is closed to hikers, but the owner is not one of the difficult variety. "It's closed?", we said. "Yes", he said, "it's closed". "So we can't pass?" we said. "It's closed", he said, gloomily, "but you just climb over the fence like everybody else does". So we did. A brief climb after the gate brings us to a T-junction of tracks just above **Coll del Olivares** (Wp.4 60M).

Bearing left at the T-junction, we continue climbing until the track levels off and we come to a large green fire-fighting reservoir (Wp.5 85M). The track bears left, dwindling to a broad trail and passing a line of cairns on our right

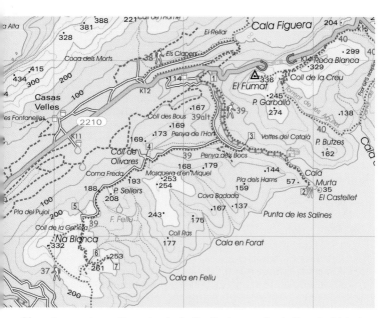

(the return route on the extension). Continuing on the trail as it skirts the south-east of **Na Blanca**, we pass several more cairns until we come to two larger cairns flanking the trail (Wp.6 95M).

We leave the trail here, turning left (SE) onto a rubble 'way' that might once have masqueraded as a track but has long since given up the unequal battle. After 75 metres, a small cairn indicates where we bear left to pick our way over sharp rocks skirting the first small top (261 metres) to cross *carritx* and dwarf palm scrubland onto the second small top (253 metres) (Wp.7 105M) from where we have fine views along the coast and into the triple gorge behind **Cala en Feliu**. Unless you wish to do the extension, return the same way except, just before the dam above Wp.3, bear left on a dirt trail to rejoin the tarmac lane a few hundred metres further up.

Extension
If you haven't already climbed **Na Blanca**, you can do so from Wp.6. Continue on the rocky trail between the two flanking cairns round the head of the **El Seller** valley. As the trail bears left on the western side of the valley, turn right on a 'way' across debris and bare rocks marked by cairns and red waymarks. Thirty metres later, bear right again to follow the cairn-marked route up to **Na Blanca** (15M from Wp.6 / see Walk 37 for a general description).

To find the cairns and waymarks down to the reservoir from **Na Blanca**, head NE, aiming between the **Morro de Catalunya** (the round pinnacle to the left) and **El Fumat** (on the right with its distinctive zigzag path), slightly favouring the **Morro**. When you see the **Casa Velles** fields, take a more easterly direction, aiming to the right of **El Fumat**. The reservoir is soon visible and all you have to do is follow the cairns along the ridge, returning to Wp.5 in roughly fifteen minutes. From here it takes about fifty minutes to return to Wp.1.

As with the **Camí de s'Alzina Fumadora** (Walk 10), **El Fumat** is said to have got its name because it was a natural place to stop and have a smoke en route from the **Cala Murta** supply boat to the **Formentor** lighthouse. Nowadays, even non-smokers are drawn to its commanding heights and it has become a well known feature of the drive along the peninsula, not least because the new road goes right through it. **Cala en Gossalba**, though surprisingly little visited, is also well known.

Our descent, however, from **El Fumat** to the *cala* via the dry **Torrent de les Agulles** doesn't appear in any other guidebook I've seen, which is quite inexplicable as it's a lovely wild little walk and makes a far more satisfying circuit than the traditional scramble over **Roca Blanca**.

Despite its intimidating aspect, **El Fumat** is a relatively easy climb, and though our descent crosses rough, pathless ground, it poses no problems so long as you're sure-footed and well-shod. The complete circuit would be a good excursion for a family with venturesome adolescents. Not recommended when it's wet or very hot.

| 3 | 2H 10M * | 6 km | 340m / 340m | ↻ | 0 |

* Short Version 1¾ h

Short Version Excluding **El Fumat**	**Stroll** To **Cala en Gossalba** and back via our return route. The path down, which isn't immediately visible from the *mirador*, starts 10 metres before the metal crash barriers on the right (direction **Cap Formentor**).

Access: by car. Park at the small *mirador* shortly before km 15 of the MA-2210. Best to get there early as there's only room for three or four cars. There's space for one car back towards the tunnel, just before the bend.

From the *mirador* (Wp.1 0M) we walk back along the road towards the tunnel, soon coming into view of **El Fumat**. 100 metres from the sign announcing the tunnel, a large wooden sign for 'Cami Vell del Far' indicates where we scramble up off the road (Wp.2 10M) on a narrow path leading to the remains of the old donkey-trail (clearly zigzagging up to **Coll de la Creu** in the distance) formerly used to supply the lighthouse. A gentle climb along the donkey trail brings us onto the *coll* (Wp.3 25M), where we see the path zigzagging down from the pass above the **Cala Murta** valley.

N.B. It is possible to reach the *coll* via the stairs on the **Pollença** side of the tunnel: this should only be attempted by men 'super, spider, or bat', as sheer drops mean one needs to be able to fly or cling to the rock like a limpet.

At the western end of the *coll*, red waymarks and cairns indicate the way up to **El Fumat**. Clear, easy walking up small patches of scree, some so well trodden it's almost a path, and sloping rock shelves, brings us to the base of the peak, where we bear left towards **Alcúdia** to follow the waymarks round the rocks to the top (Wp.4 40M).

Returning to the *coll*, we continue on the donkey trail, zigzagging down toward the head of **Torrent de les Agulles**, where there's a 50 metre level stretch, at either end of which two clear but narrow runoff channels feed into the main torrent. Leaving the path at the first of these channels (Wp.5 55M), we descend alongside the watershed, picking our way across *carritx* covered debris. We soon come to a reassuring cairn at the crux of the two runoff channels. We then follow a rough path through the *carritx*, to the junction with a second, larger runoff channel, where we take to the bed of the torrent.

Cala en Gossalba

And that's pretty much it. Unless you're feeling in an unusually perverse mood, you can't really get lost down here, and we just keep on keeping on down the torrent, hopping from rock to rock, skirting the occasional fallen pine, but always staying in or near the bed. The rocks get larger, the landscape wilder the lower we go, passing some superb rock formations as we approach the declivity of the *cala*. Within sight of the sea, we reach a final little rock shelf that's easily descended, though you may need to slide on your bottom for a moment, before eventually emerging on a tiny stony beach backed by crystal clear waters (Wp.6 100M).

To return to our starting point, we scramble onto the rocks on our left, where cairns indicate our route over to the neighbouring beach (105M). The way up from the easternmost beach is along a good path criss-crossing the **Canal de Cala en Gossalba** torrent and winding through the remains of a pine forest before climbing back to the road (130M).

Puig Sant Martí is the singular, slightly dull looking hillock behind **Playa Alcúdia**. Don't be deceived though. It's a stiff climb with some modest pathfinding problems, and the outlook on **Alcúdia**, the **Sa Pobla** plain, and the **Tramuntana** is splendid. If you're staying in **Alcúdia**, it's a must.

* Short Version 3 ** Short Version 1½h (estimated) *** in **Playa Alcúdia**

Short Version	**Stroll**
(More precisely, an easy version) in reverse, either to the smaller peak to the north, or on the easy, pathless route to the higher peak; in either case, return the same way.	To Wp.4 in reverse

Access: by car or on foot from **Playa Alcúdia**

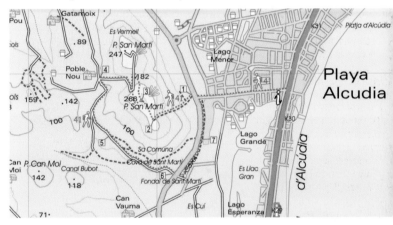

From the **Playa Alcúdia** Tourism Information Office, we follow **Avenida Pere Mas I Reus** for 800 metres past the **Bellevue** complex to the **Edificio Siesta** apartments beside the bypass. The original start of the steep climb to the *puig* has been obliterated by the bypass, but if you trace an imaginary line up from the *avenida*, you should be able to pick out the bare earth of the watercourse we follow to the top.

Crossing the bypass (traffic is sparse but fast, so take care) we scramble up the embankment just to the left of the crash barrier (Wp.1 0M) to scramble up a gap in the brush (marked with a small cairn) onto a mound of dirt. Bearing left towards a small stand of pine, we cross *carritx* and exposed rock to pick up the old path climbing to the right just before the pine. Ignoring a branch on the right, we climb towards the watercourse along a rough path studded with exposed rock and boulders. The path gets rougher and more overgrown the higher we go, obliging us to weave in and out of the watercourse, rapidly gaining height to emerge on the shallow *coll* to the left of the *puig* (Wp.2 25M). To reach the summit, we bear right on a narrow 'way' winding along the ridge, passing two cairns and a pothole, before a pathless scramble over bare rock brings us to the northern tip of the *puig* (Wp.3 35M), in view of the telecommunication towers on the smaller peak to the north. From this little eyrie we have superb views through 360°.

There are two ways to descend, one quick and perilous along something approximating a path, the other more or less pathless but considerably less precipitous. Both end on the road to the telecommunication towers. Just below us, on the western side of the *puig*, is a short denuded spur with a few pine trees halfway along its back. We descend onto the upper part of this spur.

For the quick, perilous path
We bear slightly to the right on a rough path descending directly to the U-bend in the road (not for wet weather – at the best of times it's a crab-like descent and even the big rocks are unstable).

For the gentler, pathless route
We bear right <u>below</u> the limestone rocks capping the *puig* and follow the ridge to join the road 150 metres above the U-bend.

Once on the road, we bear left and stroll down to a junction in front of a gated house (Wp.4 60M). Turning left, we follow a dirt track through the woods behind the *puig*, bearing left five minutes later at a Y-junction signposted 'Cova de Sant Martí'. The dirt track climbs gently round the southern end of the *puig*, passing a cairn-marked path to the left (Wp.5 70M; for an alternative finish you can take this path, which curves round the hillside before dropping down to go through a tunnel under the bypass and emerge at Wp.7) and, 50 metres later, another track on the left. Carrying straight on at the 'Canal d'en Bubo' T-junction (75M), we soon reach a gentle descent back to the bypass (Wp.6 80M).

Beyond the bypass, our track descends towards the lagoon, passing a large green metal cross marking the enclosed **Cova de Sant Martí** grotto. Twenty metres after the *cova*, we leave the track, bearing left on a narrow path winding through wild olive and pine woods till it's sandwiched between the bypass and a newly built slab of flats; if this path has been churned up by horse riders you can continue on the track to the metalled road.

Cova de Sant Martí

Ignoring a tunnel under the bypass (Wp.7 95M), we continue towards the **Edificio Siesta**, finally coming to a second tunnel, this time under the **Avenida Pere Mas I Reus**. The path continues toward the equestrian centre 200 metres further along, but we bear right to rejoin the *avenida*.

If doing this route in reverse
At the end of the **Avenida Pere Mas I Reus**, go to the left of the crash barriers between the by-pass junction and the **Edificio Siesta**, passing a white concrete bench and a small white building fronted with a ceramic map of Mallorca, just after which you'll find the path on your left.

Despite its proximity to one of the island's largest beach resorts, the **Alcúdia Peninsula** is a surprisingly wild place, long forsaken by man apart from the aborted **Bon Aire** *urbanización*, a small golf course, and the military installations on **Cap des Pinar**. At first glance, it can seem a bit barren, but once the eyes are used to it, there's a distinct charm to the folds of the land and the rough vegetation.

Unfortunately, the only bus service stops at **Mal Pas** and only runs in summer. Using the extension, this walk gives pedestrian access to the longer tours of the **Talaia d'Alcúdia** and **Penya Roja** (see Walks 43 & 44). It also serves as a lovely introduction to the peninsula and the island's flora, passing through a profusion of nearly all Mallorca's classic shrubs: *pistacia*, euphorbia, *carritx*, asphodel, broom, dwarf palm and more.

All three walks on the Alcúdia peninsula have now been sign and wayposted, and the approach roads are dotted with mapboards..

| 2 | 1H 20M * | 7 km ** | 260m / 260m | ↻ | 0 |

*   + 1h if walking from Alcúdia   **   + 6km f if walking from Alcúdia

Access: by car and on foot from **Alcúdia**. Motorists take the **Mal Pas** road from **Alcúdia**, turn right at the **Bodega del Sol Bar**, and follow the **Camí de la Muntanya** to the end of the tarmac at the entrance of the **Victoria Área Natural**.

If you're walking from **Alcúdia**, take the side-road just south of the Repsol Petrol Station and, after 100 metres, bear right on the lane skirting **Sa Vinya**.

Cami S'Alou

After another 100 metres, turn left on the **Camí S'Alou**. We then follow this attractive lane for 2 km until it joins the **Camí de la Muntanya**. The start of the walk is 500 metres on our right, where the tarmac ends at the entrance to the **Victoria Área Natural**. From the entrance gates (Wp.1 0M), we bear left on a broad track (see picture on the next page), climbing through the trees. After a couple of minutes, we pass a path to the right signposted **Coll de na Benet** - our return route, though if you don't have a car and want to climb the **Talaia** (Walk 43) it would be more logical to take this turning now.

Our track climbs gently then dips into a valley as it dwindles to a path with good views of **Pollença** bay.

After crossing two watercourses, we climb toward the terraced garden and large greenhouse of an enormous hilltop villa, behind which we have our first sight of the **Talaia**. We then descend alongside the **Bon Aire** *urbanización* amid a mass of shrubbery, passing a branch coming in

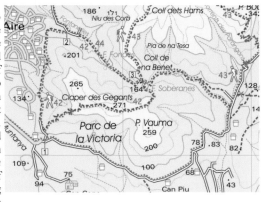

from the left, after which we gradually bear right (ENE), crossing a small rise, before joining a dirt track above the **Torrent de Fontanelles** (Wp.2 25M).

The start of the main walk

Bearing right, we cross the torrent just below a tiny dam, where we leave the track and take a signposted path up the torrent's right bank. This pleasant path, occasionally invaded by shrubbery, climbs gently alongside the torrent before crossing back onto the left bank, from where we can see the clump of trees at the **Coll de na Benet**.

Continuing our climb, we cross the torrent three times, before a final, slightly steeper ascent, brings us to the crossroads at the *coll* (Wp.3 45M). For a slightly longer walk, carry straight on here to follow Walk 43 in reverse to the **Camí de la Muntanya**; for a very long walk, turn left for the **Talaia** (see Walks 43 & 44); otherwise, we turn right.

taking a break in the **Torrent de Fontanelles**

Climbing steadily, we cross a minor *coll* from where we can see the **Illa d'Alcanada** (S), after which a final brief climb brings us over the **Claper des Gegants** knoll, within sight of **Alcúdia**'s commercial port. The path levels out and descends very slightly to skirt another knoll, after which we gradually zigzag down (as always, much further that one would expect), traversing a fallen pine and head-high euphorbia, and detouring round another fallen pine, almost immediately after which we rejoin our outward route at the 'Coll de na Benet' sign, thirty minutes from the *coll*, and two minutes from our starting point.

The **Talaia d'Alcúdia** can be a bit of a motorway, especially on the dull, 'classic' route from the north, but it's popular with good reason, boasting excellent views, both inland and out to sea. It may seem a little perverse to drive to the end of the peninsula then walk inland, but there's method to this madness as it means we can climb to the top by the little used western ridge and (subject to the safety warning; see text) end our walk with a swim.

| 4 | 2H * | 8 km | 350m / 350m | ↻ | 0 |

* + 50M for the extension

Short Version/Stroll & Extension

Platja des Coll Baix - not for the fragile or very young given the hazardous rocks and currents. Don't attempt it in flip-flops, either. At the very least, stout walking sandals or trainers are required. Also an attractive destination for a bike excursion from **Alcúdia** (ask for hire details at the Tourist Information Office).

Access: by car, bike or on foot from **Alcúdia** (see Walk 42); start as per Walk 42 and continue to the end of the **Camí de la Muntanya**. Drivers stop in the large turning circle just below the **Coll Baix** chain, cyclists at the bike-rack in the *Área Recreativa*.

From the car-park/turning circle (Wp.1 0M), we walk back along the **Camí de la Muntanya** and, shortly after a chained track to the left, turn right for 'Coll de na Benet' (Wp.2 7M) on a track alongside the bed of a dry torrent. The track peters out 150 metres later and we cross the dry torrent to take a clear, cairn-marked path climbing into mixed pine and wild olive.

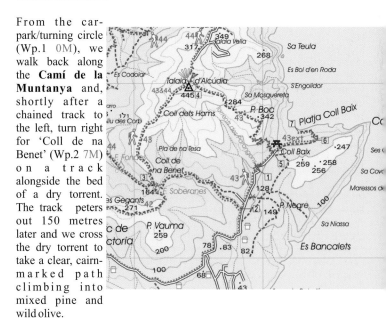

After running alongside the torrent, the path dips down, re-crossing the torrent twice, continuing through dense *carritx* and increasingly infrequent trees. After a fourth crossing, we climb away from the torrent alongside the course of an affluent, winding round a couple of fallen pine. Cairns then lead us away from the affluent along a narrow path traversing the hillside before dipping down to cross the head of the main torrent. A brief climb brings us to the crossroads at **Coll de na Benet** (Wp.3 30M), where we turn right towards the **Talaia d'Alcúdia**, which has been visible for the last ten minutes.

See Walk 44 Wps.7-11 for details of the climb to the **Talaia**. The Walk 44 waypoints have been incorporated into the GPS waypoint file of the current itinerary.

The Talaia from Coll Baix

The onward path is visible to the south. Briefly descending by the main access path (E), we turn right for 'Platja des Coll Baix' and follow a clear stony path round to the south of the **Talaia**. We then descend steadily to the watershed between **Sa Mosquereta** and the **Torrent des Parangons**, after which a gentle climb skirts **Puig Boc**. A final steep descent, tamed by innumerable hairpin bends, brings us down to the **Coll Baix Área Recreativa** (Wp.5 120M), where we can either return directly to the car or turn left for **Platja des Coll Baix**.

Extension

Gently descending through a sickly pine wood, we ignore two branches to the left and pass a large V-trunked pine, immediately after which the path briefly divides. A third branch to the left is a shortcut, but we continue to a junction where fainter traces carry straight on and the main path turns sharp left (Wp.6, 12M from Wp.5). Following the main path, we zigzag down through the trees, ignoring another shortcut near the end, 15 metres after which the path bears left on steps down to a red arrow indicating the 'way' over the rocks. We then pick our way along the rocks, keeping an eye on the alarmingly friable agglomerate to our left. It's evident from the debris that these cliffs regularly collapse, so don't venture along here after heavy rain.

Fresh rockfalls mean this section changes frequently, but at the time of writing, a roughly beaten path over the debris makes its way under a rather disturbing overhang, before we finally hop over the remaining rocks onto the beach (Wp.7 25M). We return by the same route.

WARNING: <u>This beach is notoriously dangerous</u>. The fact that the notice forbidding swimming in rough seas is in <u>five</u> languages is not merely the consequence of a casual polyglottism down the town hall.

The undertow is strong, people drown. ONLY swim here when it's dead calm, otherwise you'll be the one that's dead calm.

The scramble up **Talaia d'Alcúdia** that was the highlight of our original version of this itinerary has been cut in accordance with new conventions concerning off-path walking on the peninsula and replaced with paths (some of them a tad sketchy it must be said) used in Walks 42 & 43. To compensate, we've revised the walk to include a new start from the **S'Illot** restaurant, bumping both the belt adjustment and the refreshment rating up a couple of notches the griddled cuttlefish (sepia a la plancha) is particularly recommended. The itinerary is still the one to do if you only have time for one walk on the peninsula. The extension is highly recommended, either as part of the main walk or on its own, as per the Short Version.

Stroll: if you want a peaceful picnic spot not far from the road, descend directly into the streambed at Wp.1 and follow its course until the silence and isolation seem total.

Short Version: **Penya Roja** and **Puig Romani** from the **Ermita de la Victoria** carpark

Extension: **Penya Roja** and **Puig Romani** (see text). Add 130 metres climbing.

Access: by car, bike or (adding 3km) bus. From **Alcúdia**, take the **Mal Pas** road and follow the ermita sign to the left of the **Bodega del Sol Bar**. The walk begins at the **S'Illot** bar/restaurante, 1.5km after the **Mal Pas** bus stop.

50 metres after the restaurant, directly in front of the islet from which it takes its name, we walk up the youth hostel driveway and, 25 metres from the road, take the path off to the left (Wp.1 0M), immediately bearing right. The path climbs steadily, shadowing the driveway, then crosses a runoff channel (Wp.2 6M) where it levels out and broadens to a track.

Bearing right, we stay on the main track (SW) until it joins another, wayposted track beside a roughly concreted culvert (Wp.3 14M), where we turn right, then left 50 metres later (Wp.4) for 'Coll de na Benet, Alcúdia'. Ignoring minor branches off to the right, we follow the waymposted track towards a large hilltop villa with a lookout tower, soon bringing the folds of the **Ses Fontanelles** valley into view. We join Walk 42 (Wp.2) at a waymarked junction with a path doubling back to the right, where we carry straight on (Wp.5 27M).

The track crosses the **Ses Fontanelles** torrent beside a mini-dam and we turn right (Wp.6 29M) on a signposted path for 'Coll de na Benet'. The path climbs alongside the torrent in easy stages, crossing its course four times, before a slightly steeper ascent brings us onto the **Coll de na Benet** (Wp.7 44M), where we turn left for the ascent shared with Walk 43 (Wp.34).

At first we appear to be heading into pathless scrub, but after a few metres a faint trail (largely pioneered by goats but marked by man with cairns and the occasional red dot) becomes clear, winding through the *carritx* toward the **Talaia**, which is clearly visible for most of the ascent. A steady climb brings us to a small coll, after which the ascent becomes visibly steeper and the path dwindles to a cairn-marked way over bare rock (Wp.8 56M).

approaching the Talaia

After an initial climb along the central spine, we follow a patch of path on the southern flank, at the end of which (Wp.9 60M), we clamber across the rocks back onto the central spine. Zigzagging back and forth to break the gradient, but maintaining a northeasterly direction, we climb steeply to

view from the top

reach the foot of the summit crag (Wp.10 80M), where we can either scramble directly over the rocks onto the summit, or skirt left to join the main summit path just above a signpost indicating the descents to the *ermita* (on the left) and 'Coll Baix' (on the right) (Wp.11 87M).

Bearing left, we follow the main path as it drops through some dramatic zigzags (slippery when wet) to a stand of pine, below which the path runs into the broad track (Wp.12 95M) down to the *ermita*. Following the main track, we ignore forks descending and climbing to the right (Wp.13 & 14) and descend to a U-bend so tight it's almost a loop, above which steps and wooden railings mark the start of our extension (Wp.15 106M).

EXTENSION: The branch path climbs steadily round the northern side of the peninsula, levelling out briefly before descending then climbing alongside the crags below **Puig Romani** to a junction (Wp.16 15M from Wp.15). For **Penya Roja**, we take the path to the left, which runs alongside the cliffs to fortifications overlooking **Cap Pinar**.

Squeezing through a tunnel-like entrance, we negotiate a slightly vertiginous section (very vertiginous on the way back) with the help of a chain set in the rocks, and descend to a natural mirador amid the defensive works (Wp.17 5M from Wp.16). For **Puig Romani**, we bear right at Wp.16 and climb steeply to the **Penya des Migdia** coll, where we turn sharp right and scramble onto the summit (Wp.18 15M from Wp.16) to enjoy glorious views, including the somewhat improbable sight of a canon perched on **Penya Roja**. In both cases, we return to Wp.15 via the same route. Timings for the extension are not counted at subsequent waypoints.

To return to the start, we simply follow the main track down to the *ermita*.

Immediately before the carpark (Wp.19 116M), we turn left on the badly eroded 'Campament, Benet, Alcudia' path.

The path curls round below the carpark then descends into a densely wooded valley where it crosses the **Aladernar** torrent, immediately after which we leave the signposted path, turning right to descend into the torrent itself (Wp.20 123M), which we follow back to our starting point and a good feed.

descending the torrent at the end

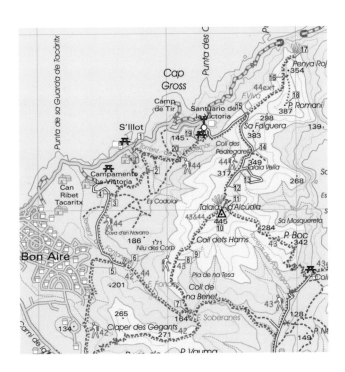

Puig d'Aguila is a firm favourite with holidaymakers, despite years of restricted access (no longer an issue), yet relatively few foreigners venture into the wilds around the more elevated summit of **La Mola**, doubtless largely because of those five little letters 'wilds'. There's nothing up there apart from us, the goats, and a lot of cairns oh, and the views, of course, which are stunning. There certainly aren't any paths for the most part, so it's pretty tough walking, but the frequent cairns are reassuring, and this might make a suitable excursion for a fit walker wanting to test themselves for the first time on rough, off-path terrain. It's very exposed, though, so don't go when it's hot and take plenty of water whatever the conditions.

Short Version: in reverse via the main track to Wps. 22, 21, or 19 particularly recommended when the low lying evening sun illuminates the Cavall Bernat cliffs.

We start from the circular **Cala Barques** carpark in **Cala de San Vicenç** (Wp.1 0M). 100 metres up the **Avenguda de Cavall Bernat,** we turn right (Wp.2) on stairs climbing to a dirt track where we bear right again (Wp.3) to reach a gate and a monument commemorating the Republican POWs whose forced labour laid the track, which would be very laudable if the monument itself didn't look distressingly like a homemade barbecue (Wp.4 6M).

Going through the small pedestrian gate on the right, we immediately leave the track, turning left on a very faint path winding through the scrub parallel to the wall. La Mola is already visible directly ahead of us. At first it seems as if we're going nowhere fast, but within 50 metres of the track, a red arrow painted on a rock indicates a cairn-marked route climbing half-right. Heading in a westerly direction and taking advantage of the patches of bare rock amid the *carritx* and dwarf palm, we climb steadily toward the back of the long sloping ridge on our right (which we follow for most of the ascent), where we pass a distinctive ball of rock, actually two fissured boulders sandwiched together (Wp.5 18M).

There are cairn-marked routes above and below here, but we favour the higher route to the right climbing onto the back of the ridge. Easy, off-path climbing brings us onto the first of two distinct rocky rises preceding the main ascent (Wp.6 32M). The obvious way up would seem to be via the long shoulder off to our left, but as we traverse the second rise and cross a scruffy coll, it

La Mola from near Wp.7

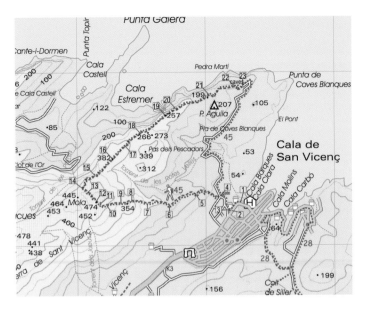

becomes clear that the main ascent is through the chaos of rock directly ahead of us, the start of which is indicated by cairns and large red waymarks (Wp.7 39M).

If you were of an uncommonly optimistic temperament, you might identify patches of trodden way here, but since they go every which way and have more to do with hoof than boot, stick with the cairn-marked route. After briefly disappearing from view, the summit comes into sight again as we cross a shallow pass (Wp.8 52M) and continue climbing to reach a coll between La Mola and a distinct rocky outcrop on our left. On the far side of the coll, cairns and a distant red waymark indicate the route for the final ascent (Wp.9 57M).

Climbing to the left of **La Mola**, we pass a solitary, rather sickly looking oleaster, bent back against the bare rock by an unequal battle with the elements (Wp.10 67M). After the tree, we climb straight up a stony gully, then bear right to reach a natural gateway in the rock (Wp.11 72M) just 50 metres short (50 fairly rough metres) of the summit, on the northern side of which you maybe blessed with a little shade (Wp.12 76M).

Cala Castell

Our return route passes to the left of the large rocky outcrop visible to the northeast, but first we descend to the north, picking our way across rough ground densely carpeted with *carritx* and shrubs to a cluster of three cairns at the head of the gully that feeds the **Torrent de les Rotes Velles** (Wp.13 85M), from where we can see a line of large cairns along the rise defining the northern side of the gully.

The walking becomes easier as we traverse more exposed rock to reach the cairn-marked rise, where fabulous views open out over **Punta Topina** and **Cala Castell** (Wp.14 88M).

Punta Galera

Bearing right, we descend along the cairn-marked route (NE), bringing into view the spectacular slender spit of **Punta Galera**.

Maintaining a north-easterly direction, we cross a distinct stony circle of reddish brown earth (Wp.15 96M) and aim for two humps of rock on a small ridge directly behind a cluster of pine trees clinging to the cliff tops. We cross the first hump (Wp.16 104M) then pass to the right of the second hump (Wp.17 108M), from where we descend half-right toward the remains of a wall below the large rocky outcrop seen from **La Mola**.

Crossing the wall via a faint trodden way (Wp.18 114M), we head for the obvious outstanding cliff top eyrie (NE), descending to a pronounced dip before climbing on what is now, to all intents and purposes, a path. After the eyrie (which is not actually **Puig d'Aguil'**, but better resembles the name than the summit itself) (Wp.19 125M), the path disappears briefly and we descend across good, firm rock to recover a rough, intermittent path (Wp.20) that weaves across a small *carritx* covered plateau to a prominent conical cairn (Wp.21 136M), the hub for several cairn-marked routes.

The main **Aguila** summit topped with a flat trig point lies off to the right, but directly ahead of us (NE) we can see a small patch of orange spoil, marking the lower **Aguila** summit. Aiming for this, we descend on an initially invisible but soon clear path along the near side of the depression between the prominent cairn and the main summit. Skirting the small **Aguila** summit with its patch of spoil and the open mouth of an old shaft (Wp.22 142M), we follow a clear path zigzagging down to join the end of the dirt track (Wp.23 145M) for a gentle stroll back to the start.

A profoundly satisfying way to conclude the new edition of this book, this splendid little summit provided one of my happiest memories of peakbagging in Mallorca. The easy climb to the foot of the mountain via **Comellar des Horts** (which features as the Short Version) takes us into one of the more privileged locations on the island that remains open to the public with unrestricted access; thereafter we venture into really wild, tough terrain for a pathless ascent that is as exciting as it is exacting. The summit itself is vertiginous and should not be approached during strong winds (a young guy got blown off last year) and, no matter what the conditions, you should tell someone where you're going. This itinerary is virtually unknown to foreigners and it is highly unlikely that you will meet anyone else up there, except for people carrying this book or, possibly, at the weekend, the odd Mallorcan. The Short Version is highly accessible and highly recommended; when you're in the tranquil **Comellar des Horts**, it's hard to believe that the busy MA2130 with its endless buses and cars ploughing up and down to **Lluc** is less than a kilometre away.

NB GPS reception is poor in the upper reaches of the valley and can only really be guaranteed by marching along holding the thing up in the air like tour guide brandishing a brolly. However, reception is good on the flanks of the mountain, where it is most useful.

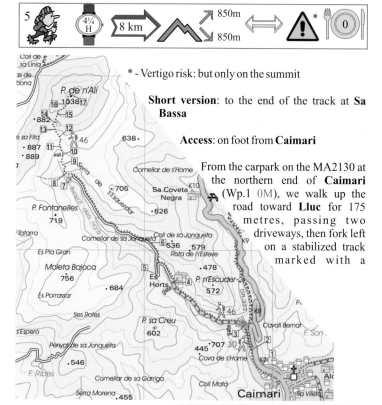

* - Vertigo risk: but only on the summit

Short version: to the end of the track at **Sa Bassa**

Access: on foot from **Caimari**

From the carpark on the MA2130 at the northern end of **Caimari** (Wp.1 0M), we walk up the road toward **Lluc** for 175 metres, passing two driveways, then fork left on a stabilized track marked with a yellow bullseye (Wp.2). 250 metres later, we go through the first of four gates (forgive the condescension, but it is essential that all gates be left as they are found, or closed if it looks like someone simply forgot) and the track becomes a narrow, surfaced lane (Wp.3).

There's no call to be reading a book after this until we reach Wp.7 as we simply follow this lane, and its continuation as a dirt track beyond the **Es Horts** farmhouses, until it ends. Passing climbing crags and impressive cavelike overhangs, we make our way into the **Es Horts** valley, a classic jumble of weathered rock, contorted olive trees and uncommonly large oak.

Waypoint 7

The tarmac ends at the **Es Horts** farmhouses (Wp.4 25M) and our steady climb continues on a rough dirt track, going through a fourth gate (Wp.5 35M), after which we are on public land. The track gets narrower the higher we go, passing cairnmarked ascents off to the right onto the **Serra de s'Equerdar** (Wp.6 41M) and left onto the **Serra de s'Esper** (55M), 100 metres after which the track ends at the attractive covered spring of **Sa Bassa** (Wp.7 57M). The *sitja* below the spring is an idyllic spot for a picnic if you're doing the Short Version.

exposed limestone

10 metres before the spring, cairns mark the easiest way onto our ongoing route, which climbs to the right then follows the watercourse above the spring. Though patches of ancient charcoalburning trails are intermittently visible, the way up to the summit is essentially offpath, traversing successive stretches of exposed, razorsharp limestone punctuated by brief forays into the woods where we cross the remains of ancient *sitjes*.

There are old blue dots and even older red arrows painted on the rock, but the best waymarks are the innumerable cairns that have been carefully placed along the line of easiest ascent.

We follow the dry streambed behind the spring, bearing right twice, first at a confluence of torrents 100 metres later (Wp.8), then after a further 100 metres (Wp.9 64M) onto the torrent's left bank, where we climb steeply amid *carritx* and fallen trees. Sticking with the cairn and waymarked route, we bear left after 75 metres to cross a rise of bare rock, at the top of which we clamber over the remains of an ancient retaining wall (Wp.10 73M) and pass to the right of an indistinct *sitja*.

50 metres above the *sitja*, we reach the foot of the first long traverse of razor sharp limestone (Wp.11 77M), at the top of which we cross another rather obscure *sitja* (Wp.12 83M). Another exposed section precedes a third, more clearly defined *sitja* (Wp.13 91M), after which the pattern is repeated, open limestone followed by a *sitja*, this time backed by the ruined walls of charcoalburner's cabin (Wp.14 96M).

Climbing steeply through the woods, we pass just to the right of an outcrop of rock and a massive boulder (Wp.15 104M), after which the faint way weaving through the woods is increasingly overgrown with *carritx*. However, we soon glimpse the summit rocks above the trees, giving us something to aim for. Zigzagging steeply up a final stretch of exposed rock, we veer right in front of an absolutely gargantuan boulder (Wp.16 118M), the overhang of which would make a good shelter in inclement weather (though what on earth anybody would be doing up here in inclement weather, I couldn't imagine!). 100 very long metres later, we scramble up to the left of the summit rocks onto the precipitous peak of **Puig de n'Ali** (Wp.17 131M).

In the unlikely event that your breath hasn't been entirely taken away by the climb, the views from the top will make short work of what remains.

summit congratulations

It is possible to descend from the far side of the summit to **Coll de sa Linia**, but I would imagine most people will have had quite enough adventure for the day, so I recommend returning the same way. Given the nature of the terrain, the descent to **Sa Bassa** should be done as slowly as the ascent, with as much care taken to follow the waymarked route, which can look very different on the way down.

See the notes on GPS use and waypoints on pages 18-19.

28.
The Siller Pass & Serra de la Punta

Wp	N	E
1	39 54.3138	3 04.6446
2	39 54.5634	3 03.9756
3	39 54.7710	3 03.6666
4	39 55.0410	3 03.4488
5	39 55.0926	3 03.7596
6	39 54.8094	3 03.5736
7	39 54.5706	3 03.3042
8	39 54.5112	3 03.2472
9	39 54.3432	3 03.3636
10	39 54.2616	3 03.4374

29. Lluc - Binifaldó - Lluc
Wp	N	E
1	39 49.2432	2 53.0832
2	39 49.4394	2 53.3820
3	39 50.0202	2 53.7234
4	39 50.1810	2 53.8182
5	39 50.5290	2 54.5898
6	39 50.0400	2 54.7272
7	39 49.6230	2 54.5082
8	39 49.4040	2 54.2544
9	39 49.7544	2 53.8470

30.
Caimari - Lluc - Caimari
Wp	N	E
1	39 46.3632	2 53.9244
2	39 46.5846	2 53.8554
3	39 46.8438	2 53.7996
4	39 47.0820	2 53.7528
5	39 47.3235	2 53.6215
6	39 47.4515	2 53.4495
7	39 47.7835	2 53.3295
8	39 47.8935	2 53.2244
9	39 47.9555	2 53.4915
10	39 48.3390	2 53.7990
11	39 48.5664	2 53.6088
12	39 48.6630	2 53.4000
13	39 48.9852	2 53.7654
14	39 49.2882	2 54.2340
15	39 49.4034	2 54.2532
16	39 49.6392	2 54.8940
17	39 49.2372	2 55.2102
18	39 49.1190	2 55.5192
19	39 49.0518	2 55.4892
20	39 48.9300	2 55.4364
21	39 48.6030	2 55.0890
22	39 48.2958	2 55.1412
23	39 48.0804	2 55.2924
24	39 47.5662	2 55.1568

31.
Puig Tomir
Wp	N	E
1	39 50.0352	2 54.7380
2	39 50.1180	2 54.9594
3	39 50.2440	2 55.0572
4	39 50.2770	2 55.1352
5	39 50.4480	2 55.3896
6	39 50.5920	2 55.5408
7	39 50.5578	2 55.7028
8	39 50.6292	2 56.0160
9	39 50.5566	2 56.3238
10	39 50.1030	2 56.4414
11	39 49.9500	2 56.1684
12	39 49.7016	2 55.8366
13	39 49.3086	2 55.5444
14	39 49.2132	2 55.2378
3208	39 49.1245	2 54.8435
3209	39 49.3475	2 54.2655
3210	39 49.3905	2 54.2475
3211	39 49.6165	2 54.5025

32.
Serra d'en Massot
Wp	N	E
1	39 50.0405	2 54.7275
2	39 49.6345	2 54.8895
3	39 49.4955	2 55.0365
4	39 49.3975	2 55.0855
5	39 49.2615	2 55.1745
6	39 49.2375	2 55.2115
7	39 49.2115	2 55.2385
8	39 49.1245	2 54.8435
9	39 49.3475	2 54.2655
10	39 49.3905	2 54.2475
11	39 49.6165	2 54.5025

33.
a Puig de María
Wp	N	E
1	39 52.3428	3 01.0200
2	39 52.0470	3 01.1844
3	39 52.1478	3 01.3530

b Fonts de Ufanes
Wp	N	E
1	39 47.5995	2 57.8085
2	39 47.6175	2 57.9075
3	39 47.9035	2 57.8205
4	39 48.2235	2 57.7225
5	39 48.2605	2 57.7545
6	39 48.3475	2 57.8125
7	39 48.4725	2 57.7905

34.
L'Havanor
Wp	N	E
1	39 52.0845	2 55.4735
2	39 52.1565	2 55.2955
3	39 52.3635	2 55.1905
4	39 52.5375	2 55.0455
5	39 52.6045	2 54.7745
6	39 52.8405	2 54.4275
7	39 52.9435	2 54.4255

35.
Rafal d'Ariant & Mortitx Gorge
Wp	N	E
1	39 52.0848	2 55.4718
2	39 52.3692	2 55.4364
3	39 52.5294	2 55.4490
4	39 52.6242	2 55.4688
5	39 52.7562	2 55.4364
6	39 53.0022	2 55.4364
7	39 53.1768	2 55.4196
8	39 53.2296	2 55.4454
9	39 53.5848	2 55.2528
10	39 53.9352	2 55.4004
11	39 53.4546	2 54.9804
12	39 53.2656	2 55.0926
13	39 53.1540	2 55.1712
14	39 52.7917	2 55.2145
15	39 52.5378	2 55.0404

36. Bóquer Valley
Wp	N	E
1	39 54.6543	3 05.1345
2	39 55.2828	3 05.2242
3	39 55.4610	3 05.4024

37.
Creek & Peak 1 - Na Blanca from Formentor
Wp	N	E
1	39 55.7100	3 08.0880
2	39 55.4874	3 09.2022
3	39 55.9314	3 08.9340

38.
Creek & Peak 2 - El Morro de Catalunya from Cala Figuera
Wp	N	E
1	39 56.8608	3 09.6810
2	39 57.1170	3 10.3812
3	39 57.4374	3 10.3782
4	39 57.4728	3 10.4322
5	39 57.6120	3 10.5666

39.
Creek & Peak 3 - Unnamed summit & Na Blanca from Cala Murta

Wp	N	E
1	39 56.9328	3 10.1784
2	39 56.2752	3 10.9794
3	39 56.4984	3 10.4466
4	39 56.4402	3 09.6576
5	39 56.1060	3 09.2196
6	39 55.8486	3 09.2370
7	39 55.8642	3 09.4140

40.
Creek & Peak 4 - El Fumat, Torrent de les Agulles, & Cala en Gossalba

Wp	N	E
1	39 57.2478	3 11.3778
2	39 57.0936	3 11.0700
3	39 56.9358	3 10.7736
4	39 56.9082	3 10.5426
5	39 56.8884	3 10.7490
6	39 56.5968	3 11.2746

41.
Puig Sant Martí

Wp	N	E
1	39 49.8774	3 06.2766
2	39 49.7358	3 05.9664
3	39 49.8522	3 05.8926
4	39 49.9650	3 05.5368
5	39 49.6464	3 05.6556
6	39 49.4406	3 06.1002
7	39 49.6002	3 06.2940

42.
Alcúdia Peninsula 1 - Ses Fontanelles

Wp	N	E
1	39 51.0684	3 09.3942
2	39 51.6936	3 09.5868
3	39 51.4014	3 10.1628

43.
Alcúdia Peninsula 2 - Coll Baix & Talaia d'Alcúdia

Wp	N	E
1	39 51.4818	3 10.9518
2	39 51.2688	3 10.8402
3	39 51.4002	3 10.1502
4408	39 51.7085	3 10.0785
4409	39 51.7735	3 10.1775
4410	39 51.9585	3 10.3925
4411	39 51.9995	3 10.4465

4	39 51.9624	3 10.4142
5	39 51.5904	3 11.0892
6	39 51.6732	3 11.4258
7	39 51.7134	3 11.3046

44.
Alcúdia 3

Wp	N	E
1	39 52.3395	3 09.7375
2	39 52.2255	3 09.8475
3	39 52.0815	3 09.5925
4	39 52.0935	3 09.5465
5	39 51.6895	3 09.5875
6	39 51.6705	3 09.6625
7	39 51.4015	3 10.1575
8	39 51.7085	3 10.0785
9	39 51.7735	3 10.1775
10	39 51.9585	3 10.3925
11	39 51.9995	3 10.4465
12	39 52.1295	3 10.4525
13	39 52.2035	3 10.5555
14	39 52.3135	3 10.6615
15	39 52.5065	3 10.6025
16	39 52.7425	3 10.9085
17	39 52.8635	3 11.0055
18	39 52.6215	3 10.9305
19	39 52.3885	3 10.2495
20	39 52.2865	3 10.0845

45.
Mola & Aguila

Wp	N	E
1	39 55.2475	3 03.2533
2	39 55.2056	3 03.2015
3	39 55.2144	3 03.1655
4	39 55.2857	3 03.0987
5	39 55.2943	3 02.9114
6	39 55.2335	3 02.6885
7	39 55.2465	3 02.5312
8	39 55.2585	3 02.4146
9	39 55.2515	3 02.3425
10	39 55.2434	3 02.2195
11	39 55.2454	3 02.1723
12	39 55.2595	3 02.1475
13	39 55.3074	3 02.0806
14	39 55.3283	3 02.0397
15	39 55.4065	3 02.1234
16	39 55.5022	3 02.2787
17	39 55.5707	3 02.3725
18	39 55.6465	3 02.4824
19	39 55.7456	3 02.6757
20	39 55.7775	3 02.7597
21	39 55.8585	3 03.0166
22	39 55.9125	3 03.2237
23	39 55.9096	3 03.2922

46.
Puig de n'Ali

Wp	N	E
1	39 46.3577	2 53.9395
2	39 46.4465	2 53.8766
3	39 46.5797	2 53.8107
4	39 46.8333	2 53.2135
5	39 46.8656	2 53.1106
6	39 47.0514	2 53.0497
7	39 47.4305	2 52.4557
8	39 47.4505	2 52.3824
9	39 47.4996	2 52.3616
10	39 47.5523	2 52.3745
11	39 47.5966	2 52.3584
12	39 47.6535	2 52.3315
13	39 47.6996	2 52.3077
14	39 47.7285	2 52.2944
15	39 47.7807	2 52.3277
16	39 47.8496	2 52.4035
17	39 47.8922	2 52.4477

This glossary contains Spanish and Catalán words found in the text (shown in *italics*) plus other local words that you may encounter. Please note that the spelling of place names and other local words on signs and maps can vary according to local conventions.

SPANISH	CATALÁN	
a		
agua, con/sin gas		water, fizzy/still
aljibe	*aljub*	ancient cistern/reservoir
alto	*dalt*	high, upper
área recreativa		picnic spot, usually with barbecues, toilets, water
atalaya		ancient watch-tower
avenida	*avinguda*	avenue
ayuntamiento	*ayuntament*	town hall
b		
bajo	*baix*	low
bajo	*avall*	lower
barranco	*barranc*	gorge, ravine
botadores		stone steps in country walls
c		
cala		creek, small bay, sometimes just a tiny coastal indentation
cala		inlet, cove
calle	*carrer*	street
camino	*camí*	road, path or way
camino real	*camí real*	royal road, once a major donkey trail
campo		countryside, field
canaleta	*siquia*	man-made water channel, including anything from a concrete canal to delicately arched aqueducts
carritx		pampas-like grass
casa	*can/ca*	house of (as *chez* in French)
casa de nieve	*casa neu*	snow pit/ice house
caseta		hut, cabin, small house
cingles		cliffs, crags; most often used to describe the sort of short, abrupt cliffs that typically define the rounded summits of many Catalán and Mallorcan mountains
ciudad	*ciutat*	city
coll		saddle, neck or pass
correos		post office
costa		coast
e		
embalse		reservoir
ermita		hermitage, small church, shrine
f		
faro		lighthouse
fiesta		festival, public holiday
finca	*lluc*	farm
forn de calc	*horno de calç*	lime kiln
fuente	*font*	spring, well
l		
lavadero		public laundry area
llano	*pla*	plain, flat land
m		
medio	*mig*	middle
mercado	*mercat*	market

mirador		viewing point, sometimes with man-made facilities, more often a natural place with a good view
morro		snout or muzzle, a rounded summit

p

parada		bus stop
particular		private
paseo	**passeig**	walkway
peatones		pedestrians
peña	**penya/penyal**	rock or boulder, used for a knoll or pinnacle on a ridge
pico	**puig**	translates as 'hill' or 'height', though more often a peak or mountain
pista		dirt road
pista forestal		forest road
playa	**platja**	beach
plaza	**plaça**	town square
pozo	**pou**	well
privado		private
prohibido el paso		no entry
puerto	**port**	port, mountain pass

r

refugio		mountain refuge, some offering basic overnight accommodation

s

santo/a	**san/sant**	saint
santuario	**santuari**	monastery, hermitage
sendero	**senda**	footpath, trail
sitja (pl. sitjes)	**sitja**	charcoal burning area or circle
su	**son, sa, ses**	his, her, their

t

tipico		typical, locals' café/bar
toro bravo		wild bull
torre		tower, often a coastal watchtower built to warn of approaching pirates, or a Moorish lookout tower
torrente	**torrent**	stream

u

urbanización		housing development

In theory, all Mallorcan bus services are now being coordinated by the TIB public transport network. In practice, private companies still publish their own timetables and some still run buses in their own livery. The following information is intended as a selective guide to the services most useful for walkers and giving a rough idea of the services' regularity at their seasonal best (between May and October). For detailed planning, see http://tib.caib.es for the TIB services (the L100s for the southwest, L200s for the central area, and L300s for the northeast) and www.autocaresmallorca.com for the Villalonga services (Linea 3 etc). Double check on arrival by asking for uptodate timetables from the Tourist Offices.

L100	Andratx Port d'Andratx s'Arrac Sant Elm	every hour or two
L102	Palma Andratx Port d'Andratx	every half hour
L111	Palma Calvi es Capdell	every 2 to 3 hours
		Sundays every 4 hours
L140	Palma Puigpunyent Galilea every 2 hours	Weekends 3 per day

NB Passengers for Galilea must book by telephoning 971 430 515 the day before.

L200	Palma Esporles Banyalbufar Estellencs	hourly
L210	Palma Valldemossa Dei S ller	every 2 hours
L211	Palma Bunyola Sóller	15 buses per day

NB There is a taxibus service to Orient from Bunyola bookable a day in advance on 971615219 or 609690553.

L320	Alar Palma (changing at Estaci Consell)	hourly
L330	Palma Selva Caimari Lluc	every 2 hours
L332	Inca Selva Caimari Lluc	every 3 hours
L340	Palma Inca Pollença	twice an hour
Linea 3	Puerto Pollença Formentor	4 times a day
Linea 4	Pollença Lluc Siller	twice a day
Linea 5	Pollença Lluc Calobra	once a day

NB Linea 5 leaves Pollença at 10.20, arrives in Lluc at 10.50, stops for an hour then reaches Calobra at 12.45. Departs for the return at 3pm, leaving Lluc at 4pm. A local website suggests passengers picking up the return bus from Lluc should be at the stop well in advance as the bus "doesn't hang about on the way back"!

For additional information on transport see:

www.mallorca.com/english
www.trasmediterranea.es
www.barcoszules.com
www.trendesoller.com

Accommodation:

Accommodation is plentiful and easily organized privately, online, over the phone or on the spot. Wellheeled walkers (and I'm not talking about your boots) favour the Hermitage in Orient (www.hermitagehotel.com), Es Mol in Dei (www.hotelesmoli.com), and s'Olivaret in Alar (www.solivaret.com). Readers of previous editions have recommended midrange accommodation in Port de S ller at the Hotel Porto S ller (www.hotelportosoller.com), Hotel Marina (www.hotelmarinasoller.com) and in Port de Pollen a at the Hostal Bahia (www.hoposa.es/pagingles/hostalbahiai.htm). For information about ermitas and refugios, see www.conselldemallorca.net and, for accommodation and food at Lluc monastery (www.lluc.net). There are no official campsites on Mallorca, but there is a designated camping area at Lluc, and camping is generally tolerated in ßrea recreativas.

www.homeholidays.com is an excellent site for booking holiday lets. Some of the properties featured are rented out at rates that suggest you're very possibly buying the place (I don't believe you are), but there are also several very reasonably priced mountain cabins and casitas de campo. Worth calling out of season when prices drop dramatically. We took a break in S ller at No. 45782 and were very pleased with the place.

Additional Information:

Emergencies   Tel. 112

www.mallorca.com/english
www.balearnet.com
www.mallorcaservice.com
www.caib.es
www.conselldemallorca.net
www.apitmallorca.com
http://idd02ucg.eresmas.net/hike.htm

Recommended addresses:

Highly recommended is the excellent Bon Cami Trekking, Outdoor and Adventure stop (Calle Roger de Flor 36, Port de Pollen a www.boncami.com). In addition to stocking a wide range of books, clothing and equipment, Suzanne and Jaume are experts on Mallorca, and may be able to advise on accessibility of routes.

Professional guide Jaume Tort's website http://idd02ucg.eresmas.net/hike.htm is a mine of information about walking in Mallorca. He can also take you on some of the more hairraising routes that it would be irresponsible to describe in a book.

Good things are said about Andy & Michelle Mitter of Tramuntana Tours (Calle de la Luna 72, S ller www.tramuntanatours.com), most excitingly that they have access to the s'Arrom estate, private land covering some classic walks that have long been out of bounds to the likes of you and me.

Calzados Bestard, c/Estaci n 4042, Lloseta are still making marvellous walking boots. If you can't make it to their factory shop, their products are available at Bon Cami (see above).

If you happen to be at the Pixarells ßrea recreativa and speak Spanish or Catalan, give our regards to Andreu, a retired lorry driver and volunteer rescue worker who spends most of the year camping out at the ßrea recreativa. Andreu 'knows nothing' about trekking, but can describe in detail every path and every summit on the island, is so engaged with nature that even his mobile phone chirrups like a partridge, and has a fund of stories about the people and places of Mallorca.

INDEX OF PLACE NAMES

Please note that the spelling of place names and other local words on signs and maps can vary according to local conventions; Castilian and Mallorquin versions are frequently different..